REAL AUSTIN

REAL AUSTIN

The Homeless and the Image of God

Annie Vocature Bullock

CASCADE *Books* · Eugene, Oregon

REAL AUSTIN
The Homeless and the Image of God

Cascade Books
An Imprint of Wipf and Stock Publishers
199 W. 8th Ave., Suite 3
Eugene, OR 97401

www.wipfandstock.com

ISBN 13: 978-1-61097-097-6

Cataloging-in-Publication data:

Bullock, Annie Vocature

    Real Austin : the homeless and the image of God / Annie Vocature Bullock.

    viii + 92 p. ; 23 cm.

    ISBN 13: 978-1-61097-097-6

    1. Homelessness—Religious aspects—Christianity. 2. Homeless persons—Biography.
3. Homeless persons—Religious life. I. Title.

BV4456 B76 2012

Manufactured in the U.S.A.

For Jennifer.

May her memory be eternal.

CONTENTS

chapter one
Real Austin

A CCORDING TO LOCAL MYTHOLOGY, the now widespread phrase "Keep Austin Weird" was coined by a man eating in an Austin-based establishment in the wee hours of the morning some years ago. As it's usually told, the man and his server chatted about the unfortunate demise of local color as chain stores and restaurants colonized the landscape. People should go out of their way to support local business, they concluded. And in Austin, the local culture is self-consciously hip, iconoclastic, even a bit subversive. In a word, it's weird. It's really weird and we'd like to keep it that way.

The slogan went on to become the trademark of the Austin Independent Business Alliance and a general rallying cry for the city. There's no question that "Keep Austin Weird" is a commercial slogan in its own right. You can find it emblazoned on T-shirts and bumper stickers, reminding you to shop local businesses: Thunderbird before a chain coffeehouse, Toy Joy ahead of a big box store, and local chain Thundercloud over a national chain sandwich shop. These choices are a point of civic pride.

Austin's weirdness is more than commercial. It's personal. Austin is a city that embraces eccentricity. There are appointed times and places for weirdness, like the array of people who turn out in costume each year for Eeyore's Birthday Party. Other times, the weirdness overflows spontaneously, like that guy who rides his bike up and down Shoal Creek in nothing but a purple G-string. Austin relishes its unusual sights. We embrace the quirks of our neighbors, even if that means a two-story yard flamingo built entirely out of scrap metal. Like junk, graffiti holds a special place in Austin's heart. Just this year, someone defaced South Austin's best-loved graffito: the phrase "I love you so much" spray-painted on the wall of Jo's, a South Congress coffeeshop, in elegant red cursive. The business owners, who do a brisk business in graffiti-themed T-shirts, carefully recreated it from photographs. Embracing local businesses is about preserving all of those local oddities that give our city character, but it's also an expression of a more general hospitality. Austinites love their city and keeping Austin weird means making everyone welcome. This sense of welcome is so lively that Austin is the kind of place where oddball people blend in instead of standing out from the crowd.

I observe these things as a relative newcomer to Austin. I came here three years ago from Atlanta, where I had spent much of my adult life. In some ways Atlanta prepared me for Austin. Genuine Southerners also have a high level of tolerance for eccentricity. As my dear friend William, a confirmed bachelor in his eighties, puts it, "We Southerners appreciate the grotesque." If I didn't want to take his word for it, I could turn to William Faulkner or Flannery O'Connor. The South—even the New South—has a touch of the Gothic about it. And I certainly knew my share of odd people, particularly through our church. I sense the same appreciation for strange things in central Austin but with an important difference. While the motley collection of off-kilter people I accumulated in Atlanta seemed to be a recognizable aspect of Southern culture at large, central Austin relishes the weird as an island of playful subversion in the vast sea of conservatism that we call Texas.

Since I've been here, I've lived with my family in a central Austin neighborhood. Our street is an uneven mix of run-down houses, mostly rental properties, and a smattering of new construction. Infill projects are common, most often taking the form of enormous ultramodern duplexes. There's a cavernous example up the street from us: an angular monstrosity with a lime green exterior. It is as bare inside as it is colorful outside. The bare white walls of the interior glare through sheets of plate glass windows. They erect an enormous Christmas tree every year, as if contractually obligated by all those windows. The rentals mostly house twentysomething hippies, alone or in packs, some of them keeping ducks or chickens. They are quiet neighbors for the most part. Through the windows of a yellow house, I can see a living room that has been outfitted with a hanging bike rack. Three or four bikes hang from the ceiling beside an old upright piano. It's out of tune but someone sits and plays rags in the evenings sometimes. A little further up, there's a vacant lot and a bus parked there. I wouldn't be surprised if someone lives in it. At the other end of the street, there's a yard full of Hula-Hoops. I saw a handwritten sign by the fence one day: "We have your bike. Didn't want it to get stolen. Just knock on the door." This is either an act of kindness or a ransom note. Either way, it's a delight.

The neighbors we know best are the homeowners we pass on our evening walk. There's a lonely man in his 70s who prays the rosary while he gardens. When we pass, he stops to introduce himself and tell us stories about cars he used to own and excellent games he once bowled. A few houses farther up, there's a young family with a little boy our son's age. They are friendly with Greg, who lives across the street. I'd hesitate to call his home a house. It's more of an art project: wrought iron, glass, and plywood housing a hearth and a workshop. He can be found out and about on his homespun motorized bicycle. His gorgeous dog, She-Ra—he adds "Princess of Power!" when he introduces her—lounges majestically in front of the ramshackle building. She's holding court nearly every time we pass.

Dory and John live next door to us in a house with bright red trim and a gator skull gracing the front flower bed. John is retired, and in good weather—which is most of the year in Austin—he can be found outside, often shirtless with a beard that reaches mid-chest. He mows lawns all up and down the street. Every week or so, he shows up at my door with something he baked, and he can be counted on to drop toys over the backyard fence for my kids. On holidays, their own kids visit and they play horseshoes in the side yard. John is proud not to own a car and even set up a "No Parking" sign in his driveway. Dory and John love Halloween above all else. We dropped in at Christmas this year with a plate of cookies and there behind the tree was a good-sized effigy of Jack Skellington, the character from Tim Burton's movie *The Nightmare Before Christmas*.

In some ways, we're the exception on this street. We aren't wealthy enough to own a home in this area. We rent an unassuming gray duplex with a dead tree in the yard. We have two bedrooms and one bathroom for five human beings and a medium-sized dog. We aren't hippies. None of us are in a band. We don't have any chickens. Instead, we're a churchgoing family with three young kids. On paper, we belong in the suburbs, the land of big lawns, safe streets, and good schools. What drew us to central Austin—and has kept us there so far—is a mix of idealism and practicality. We prefer shorter commutes so we can spend more time at home, and we chose our neighborhood for the elementary school, one of the best in Austin. Those are our ideals. The practical side is that we only own one car and that makes proximity to public transportation a necessity. We like knowing that we could manage to get the kids off to school and get ourselves to work or to the grocery store if we were without our car.

On the other side of the equation, the suburbs feel lifeless. Austin is ringed by planned communities with names like Circle C and Steiner Ranch, places with their own schools, restaurants, and spas. They may offer a feeling of safety but they also create a palpable sense of isolation. My suburban friends live in spaces that look like model homes—furniture matches, textiles coordinate. They are beautiful spaces but they require a tremendous sacrifice of time and energy to maintain. Keeping up appearances seems to go hand in hand with being Texan. The hair is done. The makeup is carefully in place. The image is perfect: a perfect wife, a perfect family, the perfect children, and a picture-perfect home. The cost in both mental and physical effort seems onerous, at least from the outside.

Central Austin is about throwing off those shackles. In that regard, living in Austin has been an unexpected blessing. I sit down to write, positioning myself between a plywood table we pulled out of someone's trash and a bookcase I bought in a secondhand store with a sign over the door advertising, simply, "Junk." Someone drew a line across one of our couch cushions with a ballpoint pen at some point, I'm not even sure when, and there are dishes in the sink. The carport is a graveyard for outgrown toys I'm planning to donate to Goodwill. There's a bag or two of clothes out there as well as an extra stroller we never use. A couple times a week, I move all the dining room chairs into the driveway because I can't figure out another way to keep my toddler from pushing them into the kitchen and using them to reach the counters. No one notices this, I'm sure. Certainly no one complains.

The practical reasons we chose this place remain. We are better off nearer to public transportation. We are comparatively close to work. My daughter loves her school dearly and breaks into the school song at random intervals. There's no denying that Austin suits us. Austin could suit almost anyone with a heart open to it.

A DOWNTOWN BUS

In many ways I was ready for Austin, prepared by Southern eccentricity. But Austin also changed me. Of all my Austin experiences, nothing has affected me more deeply than riding the 1L/1M bus through downtown. We live in North Central Austin, so my commute takes me through the heart of the city. In the beginning, I boarded the 1L/1M on North Lamar. The route follows Guadalupe—pronounced Gwad-a-loop—in front of the University of Texas-Austin. The kids call this stretch The Drag—a row of shops, businesses, and bars serving the university area. The bus continues south toward downtown, taking a left at 11th, which is the the street that passes in front of the capitol building. From there, the bus turns south onto Congress Avenue. I see protesters here sometimes. Not long ago, I saw a woman dressed as the Statue of Liberty and draped in a flag. Teachers set up a lemonade stand to protest budget cuts to the education system. I once sat on a bus for 45 minutes while the driver tried to navigate throngs of Tea Party protesters in the street. The bus follows Congress Avenue through the heart of Austin, stopping nearly every block. I see all kinds of people, from business owners to the homeless. It stops nearly every block here, passing by 6th Street, Austin's party district, until it reaches Cesar Chavez.

The bus crosses the river on the Congress Avenue Bridge, passing into the neighborhood known as SoCo—South Congress. The area is just a little bit pretentious, not unlike the Little Five Points neighborhood in Atlanta. It's a mix of old-school Austinites, who wear their cool comfortably, and the painfully hip. It's all unadulterated Austin. There are shops for used cowboy boots and a vacant lot full of food trailers serving everything from tacos to crepes. There are picnic tables here and a big waste basket with a sign that says, "Trailer Trash." We pass the Austin Motel, with its oddly phallic sign, loft-style condos, and coffee shop bars, another Austin favorite. I step off the bus at the corner of South Congress and Oltorf. There's an HEB on the corner, the local grocery chain, and a colorful array of people under the shelter of the bus stop. There are two stops closer to where I work at St. Edward's University, but I prefer to walk from here. I pass a taco shop that used to be a restaurant with a sign advertising fried chicken livers. I pass a funeral home. Once I passed some chickens on the sidewalk. When I reach the grimy corner store, I cross the street and cut through the wooded edge of campus.

This is a place where you'd find what Austinites might call urban outdoorsmen. Unlike Atlanta, the Austin Police seem relatively lenient with panhandlers. This doesn't stop the homeless from complaining about the Austin Police, but in my mind there's no question. Panhandlers are relatively rare in Atlanta. In Austin I see them at nearly every freeway exit, their makeshift signs asking for change, or prayers, or both. Groups of them congregate in open green spaces, including this one. Occasionally, I see someone asleep near the fence. Sometimes they talk to me while I'm waiting for the bus home. Most times they are gone by the time I arrive to teach my class, but I can see signs of them. I see debris, bottles, black plastic. They may not be here now but everything I see makes it clear this is where someone lives, at least some of the time.

In the beginning, I boarded at North Lamar because it was a straight shot from there to St. Edward's. I had a short walk to and from my stop and I didn't have to make any transfers. As a bus commuter in Atlanta I learned quickly that changing bus lines midstream could leave a person standing by the side of the road for an hour or more. I tried it a few times. In most cases, I gave up on the bus and walked, which is not generally the best option in Atlanta given the relative scarcity of things like sidewalks. I avoided transfers in the beginning because of my experiences in Atlanta.

The bus system in Austin is much more manageable. If you need to change buses, it's easy to do, especially downtown. And as it happens, the 5 bus runs nearer my house than the 1L/1M. A few months ago, I started taking the 5, which also runs along The Drag and through downtown. After a few semesters, I adopted a new route. I caught the 5 in front of my house and rode it downtown, changing to the 1L/1M line at the corner of Congress and Cesar Chavez.

This meant slightly less walking, which was convenient, but overall it didn't save me any time. Door to door, it was a wash. The real reason I did it, in the cold light of honest self-reflection, is that I wanted to spend less time on the 1L/1M. I radically altered my daily route in order to spend less time overall on that particular bus.

The reason I did it is pretty simple. I don't like spending that much time around homeless people. That's the honest, ugly truth. The 1L/1M is amusing sometimes. I still spend a good bit of my time updating my Facebook account with stories about my homeless co-riders. Amusing or not, the bus also smells bad and it scares me. When I'm wedged in between a hobo and another hobo and they both stink and I'm worried one of them may be strung out or crazy, I think about the long list of places I'd rather be, starting with anywhere.

STARING SIN IN THE FACE

My reluctance to share space with the homeless is out of line with Austin's spirit of freewheeling acceptance. It's also out of line with the spirit of Christian charity. It demonstrates unequivocally my failure to respond lovingly to people—real human beings—whose situations and hygiene practices happen to offend me. The cold fact is that I substantially altered my bus route to avoid the smell of an unwashed body. In this visible, concrete way, I arrange my life so that I interact as little as possible with people who are unlike me.

I could excuse myself by insisting that this is only natural. That would be a lie. It's a tempting lie. That doesn't make it helpful or true. It's never helpful to excuse my failings if humility is my goal.

Humility requires self-scrutiny. The most helpful practice, in that case, is to admit my failings and call them to mind over and over. No matter how it sounds to modern ears, this isn't an invitation to self-loathing. On the contrary, humility requires honesty, and if I'm being honest I have to acknowledge that I'm not different from other people. I am no better than others but I'm also not a special study in failure and sin. I deserve no accolades, but neither do I deserve any particular or disproportionate blame. Self-scrutiny is most helpful when it's honest. And in this case, it is both helpful and true to admit that my desire to avoid the homeless is a failing. My homeless avoidance strategy is an excellent example of my failure to look humanity in the eye and love it anyway. In other words, it is sin.

The emphasis on sin that runs throughout this book may seem out of place. I operate in a theological culture that gives limited space to concepts like sin and judgment. This is a good thing insofar as it undermines the tendency to use sin as a bludgeon. It's not for nothing that we joke about Roman Catholic guilt or Christians who are too afraid of hell to enjoy life, let alone extend compassion to those who are anything less than perfect. Holier than thou is a cliché because it's true. An obsessive fixation on sin as personal guilt is deleterious to spiritual life. It binds rather than frees.

It's also the case that too much emphasis on sin and judgment spills over into pride. Sin is something other people do. The deeds of the wicked function as a cautionary tale. It's often a pretty outlandish tale. I grew up with stories of boys and girls who fiddled with Ouija boards as kids and found themselves ritually sacrificing the family cat before anybody could stop it. I learned that anybody who goes into a bar or hangs around in one is likely to become a drunk, to sleep around, or to beat the kids. And I learned that gay people were sexually deviant, not only in their desire to sleep with someone of the same sex but because indulging that desire led to sadomasochism, erotic humiliation, and orgies. These were not, of course, anything anyone in our congregation would ever do. The emphasis was on not taking that first step down these terrifying paths.

This tendency, so familiar from my childhood, is apparent in the documentary *Hell House*, which follows the work of a Cedar Hill, Texas, church in putting on a haunted house that subjects visitors to scenes that depict the horrors of sin and hell. These scenes rest on the same premise that small sins lead to greater evils and finally death, at which point the demons arrive to drag the already miserable sinner to hell. There are touching moments in the film as well as disturbing moments, but there's also an unintentionally funny exchange between a pair of scriptwriters who can't figure out the proper title for a trading card game called *Magic: The Gathering*. The game was a persistent feature of my band-geek adolescence. But for the folks in Cedar Hill, it's a lot like *Dungeons & Dragons* and *Harry Potter* in being the first step on a path that leads to Satanism. What's funny is that scriptwriters can't decide how to refer to the game because they obviously don't know anything about it. It follows that their hell house scenes are a caricature of "evils" they've never seen or experienced. This is all because sin, as they think of it, arises in the lives of people from bad homes who make poor choices. In other words, sin doesn't happen to people like us.

The exchange is comical but the results are gut-wrenching. In what is for me the most difficult scene in the entire documentary, visitors to the hell house watch a young woman enact committing suicide. Her fictional backstory is that she was sexually abused by her father, which manifested in later promiscuity, as it often does in real-life cases. The young woman has attended a rave, done ecstasy, and been gang-raped. In a fit of despair and urged on by a demon—another actor in a plastic mask—she slits her wrists. Moments later, the demon drags her to hell.

There is no empathy. There is no mercy. She is responsible for every choice. The writers had enough insight to connect her behavior with a troubled history. Even that doesn't matter. She is punished by a God whose judgments are simple in the extreme.

This is the theology of sin gone horribly awry but not because there is no sin in the story of this imaginary woman. There is sin in the actions of her father. There is the sin of the men who raped her. And I would even say there is sin in the young woman's own behavior. She is caught in a downward spiral of self-destruction. In Romans, Paul says the wages of sin is death. I was raised to read this as a statement about the afterlife but it just as easily describes the way sinful patterns of behavior wreak destruction in this life. The sins of the father are visited upon his daughter, who is driven by sin to the point of despair. Where the hell house version of the story goes wrong is in its vision of God's judgment. The God of hell house does not make God's bed in Sheol with a bruised, broken, suffering woman, torn apart by the ravages of sin. The God of hell house punishes without any reference to justice and certainly without mercy. Why should God condemn a dying soul to hell when that soul is already living in hell?

These errors are real but it doesn't help downplay the role of personal sin. Personal sin is too much a part of the human story. Ron Sider makes the important observation that there is a kind of split in Christianity, reflected now in the split between evangelical and post-evangelical thought, on the nature of sin and salvation. On the one hand, there are those who emphasize evangelism and conversion, which requires greater attention to issues of personal sin, judgment, and even hell. Against that, others emphasize social justice and therefore focus on collective or systemic sin. Sider observes that both personal and systemic sin are in fact points of biblical emphasis and yet "each group uses the other's one-sidedness to justify its own continuing lack of balance, and the division devastates the church's witness and credibility."[1] What folks on both sides of this opposition have in common is the overwhelming tendency to refer sin outward. This is just as true of systemic sin as it is of personal sin. Naming a sinful system is easier than identifying my own complicity in it. Listing personal sins and describing paths of destruction is far easier than considering the many sinful patterns of thought and action in my own life. Most of us are quite comfortable laying out, often in great detail, the failings of other people, people who are largely not like us. Progressive Christians are no less guilty of this than fundamentalists. We use our cherished issues to cover for it.

There is something powerful in retrieving personal sin for the purpose of looking at my own sin and not the sins of anyone else. This is a check on the danger that this talk of sin will turn abusive or restrictive. The locus of accusation is fixed firmly and clearly in the self. That is the place of sin in this book. It functions as a template for critical self-examination. It is a theological means to evaluate my own way of being in the world and to determine if it is Christian after all. And finding that it is not, as I am sure to discover, naming this way of being sin is a call to change.

1. Sider, *Good News*, 17.

GIVE ME A WORD

I come by my concern with sin honestly. Like I said, I grew up a funda-
mentalist. What this means in practical terms is that I've asked Jesus to
come into my heart at least three dozen times, and I've recommitted my
life to Jesus at least that many. I couldn't put a number on the many times
I said a quick prayer for forgiveness of sins, just in case a bus hit me the
next moment. I was baptized at the tender age of six. This didn't quite
meet the age of reason in our congregation, so it only happened after I
insisted, tromping to the front of the church week after week at the altar
call. I wouldn't say I was afraid of hell exactly—hell is for other people,
after all—but I did believe in it and I certainly thought it was important to
get right with God. As many times as it took.

I'm still just as concerned about getting right with God, but things
have changed. My desire to confront sin at this point is fueled more by my
conviction that what's uncomfortable is spiritually valuable. My conviction that it is spiritually beneficial to take an honest account of our failings
springs from a long engagement with the Abbas and Ammas—fourth-
and fifth-century men and women who retreated to the desert to pray and
more or less stopped bathing. I first read Athanasius's Life of St. Anthony
as a graduate student and fell in love with Anthony and Athanasius
at the same time. I'm attracted to the bizarre and Anthony is nothing
short of that epithet—not wasting but thriving in spite of his asceticism.
Athanasius describes the state of his teeth at death, worn down but none
missing. This commentary on Anthony's oral hygiene underscores the
visceral reality of Anthony's religion. Anthony disciplines body and soul,
not as distinct realities but as seamless parts of a single whole. He wrestles
against spiritual enemies but the manifestations Athanasius describes are
equal parts spiritual and physical. We find Anthony at home among the
tombs or locked away in a fortress but always wrestling with demons,
body and soul. The bodies of the demons are light and airy, subtle and yet
substantial. Like Anthony, they are one thing, both physical and spiritual.
There is no separation between the physical and spiritual, this world and
that other world. It is all one thing: reality. But it's reality as we are unaccustomed to recognizing it. It is little wonder Anthony's story inspired
the surrealist painter Salvador Dali—Dali's characteristic spindle-legged
horses and elephants march as they bear gilded, bare-breasted temptation
and Anthony stands in the foreground, naked and sinewy, a makeshift
cross in his hand and a skull at his foot. Anthony and his compatriots

are the roots of Christian monasticism: a raggedy group of mostly illiterate hermits living on the edges of civilization, saying little and writing absolutely nothing.

It's a little bit remarkable that we know as much as we do about the lives and words of the Abbas and Ammas, also known as the desert fathers and mothers. Some of them were educated but many others were not and none of them spent their time writing. There were others who wrote about them—just as Athanasius wrote an account of the life of Anthony the Great—and collected their words of wisdom. These wise words were gathered in collections of sayings, which are available to modern people even if they aren't always easily accessible.

The basic structure of early monastic life is apparent in the sayings themselves. The desert fathers and mothers lived alone—in caves or small shelters they called cells—but they had contact with one another. The sayings record stories of their lives alone. They speak of long hours uninterrupted by nothing but prayer and the burden of loneliness and boredom that came with them. But there was also community in the midst of solitude. The sayings also record questions from one Abba or Amma to another and advice about how to bear with one another's faults. They fled from the social fabric of city life, and in the process, they founded a new kind of city in the desert—a counter-society with its own norms and problems.[2]

Nearly all of the Abbas and Ammas warn about the dangers of too much contact with other people and extol the value of solitude. At the same time, it's extremely common for sayings to begin either with a question about a specific issue or with a simple request: Abba (or Amma), give me a word. This is how the novice, looking for wisdom, approached the master. What followed was typically something hard or puzzling. The word is frequently counterintuitive. These sayings are almost like Zen koans. They are designed to offend the sensibilities of a beginner and force her to reconsider everything she used to think was obvious. They disconcert rather than comfort. The beginner seeks a word and returns with it to her cell to wrestle with its truth.

Even though they stood at the margins of society, the Abbas and Ammas acquired significant social and moral authority. Peter Brown explores this apparent paradox in a classic essay on the role of the holy

2. For more information about the desert fathers and mothers and their way of life see Chitty, *Desert a City*; Burton-Christie, *Word in the Desert*; and Elm, *Virgins of God*.

man (or woman) in late antique society. According to Brown, the fact that the holy man removed himself from society secured his place in that society. The holy man's move into the desert symbolized his rejection of everything ordinary men and women value—from putting away money and goods in preparation for old age to bathing on a regular basis. It's not uncommon to be attracted to those who reject us. This is the beginning of the holy man's mystique.[3] The holy man's rejection of the world was theologically motivated. Moving to the desert placed him in solidarity with Christ. This cemented his place in Christian imagination. The move into the desert redefined the holy man's relationship to the social order. By aligning himself with Christ in the same move, the holy man was no longer a part of the world but rather stood in judgment over it.

For the most part, the Abbas and Ammas rejected this role and continued to flee from the world. There are abundant stories of holy men and women who refused to receive visitors or treated them harshly. But of course this only heightened the attraction. The farther they ran, the more urgently they were followed. And throughout the collections of sayings left to us, there are stories of wealthy and powerful men and women who clearly looked to the desert for guidance.

If I didn't understand this impulse perfectly, I doubt I would be writing this book. I will admit that the idea of taking my cues from a lot of long-dead people who lived in caves in the desert and probably wouldn't talk to me if I met them is a little bit implausible. I don't live in the desert, for one thing. For another, my life couldn't be more different from the average desert father or mother. They were celibate and I am married. They gave their lives to prayer and simple manual labor. I live in a duplex in a mid-sized city with too many people and my work is about as far from manual labor as it can get. I sit and think. I write. I read. They fled from the world and I seek it—through my writing, through social media, and in the classroom. I'm fairly sure they'd frown on my extensive education, too, if I gave them a chance. There's even a saying condemning the practice of owning books when the money they cost could be used for the poor.[4] Let's just say that while I give to the poor, I own more than a few books. I'm not sure most of the Abbas and Ammas would like me very much, let alone take me on as a student.

---

3. Brown, "Holy Man," *Journal of Roman Studies*, 80-101. Brown published an updated version of the essay in 1998, which took account of additional research.

4. *Sayings*, 227.

There are times when I don't really even like the desert fathers and mothers, let alone want to emulate them. They're strange to the point of being inscrutable and they can be harsh. Some of the time, I can't even make sense of what they're doing. There's a story about Abba Isaac, who ate the ashes from the incense with his bread.[5] There are stories about monks and virgins who are praised for not noticing their physical surroundings at all.[6] And then there are implausible stories that seem like extremes of bodily mortification and asceticism. I'm not sure I really believe that Abba Bessarion stood upright in a thornbush for fourteen days without sleeping and even if I did, I'm not sure I think that was such a good idea.[7] Of course, there are limits. One of my favorites stories is about Abba Sisoes. In an attempt to overcome sleep he hung himself on the side of a cliff like some sort of deranged Prometheus. Goodness knows how long he would have lasted but "an angel came to take him down and ordered him not to do that again and not to transmit the teaching to others."[8] The function of this story is pretty clear in a tradition that supports stories like the one about Abba Bessarion in a thornbush. Push yourself to the edge but don't go over.

THE URBAN DESERT

The desert material is powerful because it stands at the margins. The margins are always powerful if not always comfortable places. I recognize this. As often as I can, I remind my students that if they don't hate the assigned reading, it probably isn't what they really need to read. It is easy, after all, to continue to read the things that comfort us and confirm us in easy patterns of thought. It is pleasing but it isn't necessarily productive. Growth and change are painful, but the pain of growth is positive. It generates rather than destroys.

In the spirit of pushing myself to the limit of what I can bear, I'm choosing to face the things that still disconcert me. I have made friends with the Ammas and Abbas but if I take them at their word, I will never be finished identifying my failures. In fact, I cannot choose another direction until I've recognized my own sin. And in seeking my own sinfulness,

5. Ibid., 100.
6. Ibid., 62, 230.
7. Ibid., 42.
8. Ibid., 219.

I'm pressed out into the world and to the margins of my own community. And living at the margins of my urban desert, there are men and women who reject the norms of ordinary society—by choice or by necessity—who challenge me. They challenge me so heartily that I arranged my route to work so that I could spend as little time as possible among them. I call this sin. It is the most ordinary kind of sin there is.

The men and women who live on Austin's streets are a motley collection. They are as diverse as any other community. Each is, after all, an individual. They do have a common way of life in a basic sense. By choice or circumstance, with or without the mitigating factors of addiction or illness, all of them survive with little or no income and without a permanent place to call home. Their lives are about survival strategies, even if the particulars of their situations differ. Their common life amounts to a kind of culture. There are even discernible differences in lifestyles by neighborhood. The kids who live on The Drag tend to carry their gear in backpacks. They are young and I see many who keep dogs on leashes or tied to ropes. They are a world away from the men I meet on South Congress, who keep their belongings in plastic sacks from HEB or who carry little with them, having stashed it somewhere else, sometimes in an apparent effort to pass for the non-homeless. They are older than the kids on The Drag. They are more worn and more likely to reek of alcohol. On the whole, they smell worse.

I changed my route to avoid all of them. I did this because they scare me, they offend me, and they repulse me. This is the sin. It is a sin because when I reduce them to their circumstances, I elevate myself and I belittle them—even if only in my mind. It is a sin because when I think of them as a situation to avoid, they are no longer human to me. They are no longer beings in the image of God. So long as I fail to recognize their humanity, I am incapable of seeing them as they are, let alone loving them.

When I think of people who live outside, wear rags, and stop bathing, I think of the desert. When I think of the desert, I remember my sin. And here two margins collide. This is where my easy, comfortable acceptance of the hard, wise truths conveyed by the Abbas and Ammas meets the lived reality of my days on a downtown bus. I need a word in the urban desert.

chapter two
Everybody's Favorite
Homeless Transvestite

Abba, give me a word.

Abba Poeman said, "Not understanding what has happened prevents us from going on to do something better."[1]

WHENEVER I MENTION THE homeless in Austin, the first name on everyone's lips is Leslie Cochran. It seems like almost everybody has a Leslie story. Mine dates from my first weekend in Austin. My husband was about to start graduate school at the University of Texas and we were in town looking for housing. We were driving down Sixth Street in search of something to eat when I saw Leslie on a corner. He was wearing a denim miniskirt and a tank top, a bandana over his greasy white hair. He was waiting to cross the street, and when the light turned, he wandered into the road. Halfway across, he faltered, turned back to the curb he had just left and casually slung his skirt over his hips, revealing a purple thong. I posted the story to Facebook and within 90 seconds, I had a comment from a friend. "That's Leslie," he wrote. "Welcome to Austin!"

I've never encountered Leslie on the bus. In fact, until relatively recently, I'd never met him. Leslie's status as an Austin icon is undisputed. He's a symbol of the freedom of expression and creativity prized by so many. There is an iLeslie app for iPhone, and Book People, a local Austin retailer, carries a magnetic Leslie dress-up doll. He has a column in *The Challenger*, a local street newspaper, called "Leslie's Korner." Leslie's corner, everyone knows, is Sixth and Congress. This information is related in his Wikipedia entry. He is not Austin's only homeless person with a Wikipedia entry but he is likely the most beloved.

1. *Sayings*, 194.

Leslie's appeal is that he moves through the world on his own terms. He is homeless but he doesn't think of himself that way. He finds himself on the wrong side of the law but he presents himself as a stand-up guy. As far as he's concerned, there are ideals that are bigger than the petty concerns of the Austin Police Department. He may get arrested or harassed by small-minded lawmen but that doesn't make him a criminal. He's an outlaw, like the heroes of the Westerns he loves so much, a lone man against the elements with only the strength of his own character to sustain him.

Leslie's place on the margins of Austin society gives him a similar mystique. He is not very much like the heroes of Westerns in his manner of life, of course, but he is like them in that everyone wants to know his story. Where does he come from and where does he sleep? These are the questions people asked about Anthony of Egypt or Daniel the Stylite. By Athanasius's account, Anthony spent some of his time living in a graveyard before moving to an abandoned fortress.[2] And Daniel the Stylite lived high on a platform at the top of a pillar. He takes his epithet from his predecessor, Simeon Stylites, from whom he learned his bizarre way of life. According to his biographer, he spent most of his time standing, causing extreme pain in his feet, and he refused to allow anyone to build him a shelter, even after he nearly froze to death in a storm on the banks of the Bosphorus where his pillar stood.[3] Is it crazier that Daniel would do such a thing or that he wasn't the first one to try it? We ask because we want to know how a person could make such a radical choice. Are they crazy? Is he some sort of addict? Is there a mental illness we can diagnose? Or is he that much more committed to his spiritual life?

Ironically, people ask a similar set of questions about Leslie. It's not clear if he's a drunk or a junkie or if maybe he's just mentally ill. Whatever odd configuration of factors prompted him, he's living a life that is unlike the one any of us lead and we admire him for it. He has the quality of a living legend. Wikipedia lists 1951 as his birth date but even this is probably not certain. The rest of the information provided is mostly a smattering of stories Leslie told someone at *The Austin American-Statesman* at some point. His stories are as colorful as he is and they add to his appeal. It doesn't really matter if he ever rode a three-wheeled bicycle cross-country or skinned road kill in Colorado. We'd like to think he did. Like those holy men and women, his place on the margins gives him some authority

2. Athanasius, *Life of Anthony*, 37-41.

3. Doran, *Simeon Stylites*; Dawes and Baynes, *Three Byzantine Saints*.

as a truth-teller. In his column in *The Challenger,* he calls the police to account for their practice of arresting homeless men and assigning them community service. Not only that, but he has been known to expose the hypocrisy of Christians who profess their faith in Jesus Christ—a man who reached out to the poor—and yet escort the homeless to the door as soon as they enter the building. Leslie tells the truth fearlessly because he doesn't have anything to lose if he does.

I met Leslie face to face for the first time not long ago at his sixtieth birthday party. The party was held at Threadgill's, on West Riverside. When I arrived, Leslie was standing near the entrance. A mostly young crowd was busy filing into the beer garden, paying the $10 cover on the way. The party looked like a cross between an informal concert and a wedding reception. Drinks were available for purchase at the back. Toward the front, folding chairs were set up in front of the stage. Local Austin blueswoman Toni Price was prepared to perform and people were milling around in small groups, chatting happily.

Leslie turned toward me just as I walked up. He was wearing a black tank top and a zebra-print skirt. "Thank you all so much for coming," he said. Then he made a grand sweeping gesture with his arms, tucked one foot behind the other in a kind of half-curtsy, took my hand, and kissed it.

Twenty minutes earlier, I had been at home in front of the mirror trying to decide which earrings to wear. What do you wear to the sixtieth birthday party of a homeless man you've never met? I had no template for this sort of event. I really had no idea who would be there. I noticed after I arrived that the crowd—which generally skewed young and hip—included no homeless people. This was, of course, my chief question and concern as I fretted about how to dress and what to bring. I was anxious for the simple reason that I was afraid. This was unknown and I was going alone. More to the point, I had an unsettled feeling that I could find myself socializing with crazy people.

AN UNCERTAIN AND TERRIBLE CERTAINTY

I use the word "crazy" here under advisement. "Mentally ill" is a more appropriate term for what I mean but "crazy" captures my irrationality about it. It's a truism that a significant proportion of the homeless are people with untreated mental illnesses. I know that some portion of those are people with unmedicated schizophrenia. I am skittish about this and

I come by it honestly. Everything starts at home and this, too, is rooted in childhood and adolescence.

My mother married Johnny's father when I was nine years old and he was eleven. Johnny was a string bean of a kid—lanky with a mop of black hair over his olive complexion. He was ordinary in most ways. He was quiet and kept to himself. He read a great deal. He was a good student —the kind teachers considered a real pleasure to have in class. I liked him. He resisted the idea of a blended family but we were fast friends all the same. We spent our time on PC adventure games, play-acting improvised zombie movies, and listening to LL Cool J. That was before he got sick, before I knew about his schizophrenia.

There was a kind of sadness about him that had roots in his parents' divorce—a separation that came as a direct result of his mother's illness. She was schizophrenic, too. When it became clear that she would be hospitalized for an indefinite period of time, her parents encouraged their son-in-law to move on with his life. He eventually joined a dating service and met my mother. They bonded over single parenthood and Chinese food and less than a year later, they were married and I thought of him as my Pop.

I was afraid of Johnny's mother when I was a little girl, more for the stories I'd heard about her than for anything she did the few times I met her. She once put a candlestick through a wall, I was told. The paint was ever so slightly a different color there. There was a picture in an album of Johnny at about three years old with blond hair instead of black. She dyed his hair blond for the first five years of his life without anyone knowing it. My mom complained about the debts. Johnny's mother took cabs to the department store downtown. This itself was noteworthy because my hometown is a relatively small place and taxi cabs are uncommon. But the real story was the enormous debt she incurred shopping. She couldn't keep a job. She didn't keep the house. She once had crumbs on her blouse and she didn't notice for an entire afternoon.

She was my first introduction to that great gray area that is mental illness. So much of what seemed strange about Jill wasn't really very strange at all. Some of the stories were troubling—like the story about the candlestick—but others, her overspending or the crumbs on her blouse, didn't seem to amount to much on their own. Even in the inevitable scheme of fault-listing that accompanies divorce, Jill's stated problems seemed mild. They certainly didn't seem like a clear indication of mental illness.

In person, she was equally benign. She was pleasant and accommo-dating, a pretty, willowy blonde woman with a wispy, singsong voice. If anything seemed strange about her, it was her voice. It sounded young, even juvenile. And she fawned over Johnny in a way that made me un-comfortable. I wouldn't say I liked Jill but I wouldn't say she seemed that sick, either—certainly not sick enough to be in a hospital.

But she was sick, on the other hand, and desperately so. I heard tell that she was as sick with schizophrenia as her doctors had seen. Even with medication, she didn't function well. And I can't deny that in hindsight there was something unsettling about Jill. There was a kind of indefinable quality she had that made her seem off, if only ever so slightly. As I got older, I was privy to a few more stories. Jill thought she was having an affair with the next-door neighbor—much to the chagrin of both the man and his wife, neither of whom had ever said more than two words to her. She used to say Johnny was John the Baptist reincarnated. I overheard a story about a phone call she made to Johnny to tell him that his father had cut out her cervix. I never heard any explanation.

The point isn't that Jill wasn't actually sick. She was. But her illness had the kind of subtle, banal character that is the hallmark of day-to-day mental illness. In popular culture, mental illness is frequently stigmatized, and as a corollary, it is frequently dramatized. Mental illness is often pre-sented as a cut-and-dried issue. In fictional accounts, people are crazy or they aren't. When Lucia di Lammermoor, in Donizetti's opera, wanders into the party soaked in blood and in a world of her own, there's no ques-tion about her mental state. There's no wondering if she is or she isn't. There's no worrying about the crumbs on her blouse. Her madness is frightening or pathetic but it isn't ambiguous.

The Romantic notion of madness as a reverie is somewhat out of fashion now. Dame Joan Sutherland played Lucia as a woman lost in a trance. She thinks she really is marrying her beloved when in fact she has already been married to another, murdered him in their marriage bed, and wandered back out into full view of the party covered in his blood. She is unaware of this—a woman out of touch with the hardness of an ugly reality and instead immersed in a dream. Sutherland's voicing was gentle, beautiful, even ethereal. She is a woman too weak-minded to cope with her circumstances.[4]

4. Donizetti, *Lucia*, 2006.

Anna Netrebko's sensitive portrayal of Lucia suggests something entirely more modern. She projects resourcefulness. Her mind is not the frail organ of a weak woman. Her retreat from reality projects the incredible strength of a woman to endure psychologically by whatever means necessary. She is a pathetic figure, in the best sense of the term, and we are invited not only to pity her but to find ourselves in her. The terror is not that she is lost in a dreamworld. Netrebko's Lucia reads as a woman on the razor's edge of realizing the truth about what she has just done.[5]

This new Lucia offers the audience an opportunity to experience and subvert a fundamental anxiety. We project ourselves into her position and experience the anxious thought that we might be capable of murder, then return to ourselves and feel sorry for her death. In fact, we are experiencing the anxious thought that we, too, might be ill. There is a kind of ambiguity about her madness that matches the ambiguity of real mental illness and betrays our fear that we, too, might be just as sick. Sutherland's Lucia presumes the hard objective reality of a world beyond ourselves and it polarizes the sane and the insane. There is no mistaking Lucia and, although we pity her, we can be comforted to know that she is not us. A postmodern Lucia troubles all those certainties.

The film *Donnie Darko* invites the audience into the same space between madness and reason. As played by Jake Gyllenhall, Donnie inhabits this liminal region as if caught between states of sleeping and waking. Donnie's therapist ultimately diagnoses him with schizophrenia and his hold on reality seems increasingly tenuous as the story progresses—at least as far as we can assume that a man in a bunny suit is not actually a harbinger of the end of the world. Nothing is certain. Is he or isn't he? The terror is heightened by our identification with him. The film can be read either way, although a straightforward interpretation suggests that Donnie is perfectly sane. The visual world of the film is almost surreal. The audience recognizes the sights and sounds of suburban American life and yet as Donnie peers behind the veneer of the world, nothing is familiar anymore. Donnie's story is a single, extended experience of *jamais vu*, where nothing familiar seems recognizable anymore. The audience has the same experience when the director finally reveals the truth about his characters. Everything we have learned about the characters and their relationships is subverted. The final montage pans across the faces of characters we're no longer sure we know, to the strains of a poignant, familiar song about

5. Donizetti, *Lucia*, 2009.

dreams—significantly, a recognizable song covered by an unfamiliar artist. The overall effect is uncanny.

I saw *Donnie Darko* for the first time in the middle of a Tuesday afternoon. A friend showed up at my door with a copy of the film insisting that I needed to see it. We settled in to watch it together and I quickly fixed on Donnie's sister, Samantha, the character with whom I most identified. Samantha is a completely ordinary child and devoted to her older brother. In what is for me a pivotal moment, Donnie is deep in conversation with Frank—the bunny-suited horseman of the apocalypse—when Samantha appears in the doorway. She asks him a simple question that contains all the poignancy of my experience of my brother's illness: "Who are you talking to?"[6]

What writer/director Richard Kelly conveys so well is that the descent into mental illness is a deeply ambiguous process for all involved. Some of Donnie's actions and beliefs seem undeniably psychotic—as for example his bathroom conferences with Frank. Others have a kind of sublime rationality. His public confrontation with Jim Cunningham, brilliantly played by Patrick Swayze, is a good example. Although his outburst is construed negatively by the ostensibly right-minded adults in the room, the audience—both on and off the screen—cheers him on. Later when he exposes Cunningham as a pedophile, Donnie is morally vindicated. He sees people like Cunningham for who they are, even if no one else does. If he's right about Cunningham, who is to say he isn't also right about Frank? Is he out of touch with the real or are we?

In the world of the film and in life, sometimes it's hard to tell. On that Tuesday afternoon watching the film for the first time, I heard Samantha ask her brother who he was talking to and I laughed out loud. My friend snapped to attention and gave me an unsettled look. I burst into tears. This confusion of emotion characterizes my memories of my brother's illness. Viktor Frankl attributes abnormal responses to normal men and women in deeply abnormal circumstances and there may be something of that here. In this case the act of recalling a deeply abnormal situation produced an unusual response: laughter. It wasn't funny. I knew that. I laughed but the laugh contained all the confusion, pain, and sadness of a certain uncertainty: something is wrong and I don't know what it is. And that's why I cried.

6. "Emergency PTA Meeting," *Donnie Darko.*

By the time I was twelve, it seemed pretty clear there was something wrong with Johnny. He was withdrawn. He seemed more reserved than usual. Where he used to participate in family activities, he spent longer and longer periods of time in his room. There was reason for concern, although nothing on the surface that would suggest mental illness.

We were a deeply religious family and the first set of conversations I remember had to do with spiritual forces. My mother and stepfather thought there could be something dark in him, maybe something invited by his interest in *Dungeons & Dragons*. None of us had ever played *Dungeons & Dragons*. We weren't allowed any more than we would have been allowed to hold a séance using a Ouija board. But Johnny did read fantasy novels including some set in the same imaginary world as *Dungeons & Dragons*. Demonic activity was a possibility that particularly frightened me because I had a strong sense of the reality of things unseen and because I had read all the same books as Johnny.

Johnny's doctors thought his retreat could be situational. We were a blended family, after all, and blended family dynamics can be difficult. Johnny didn't have a very good relationship with his own mother because of her illness, which had been worse recently. He also didn't have a very close relationship with my mother. It seemed possible that this could be behind his behavior. We attended a few sessions of family therapy to discuss things but nothing seemed to come of it.

What everyone suspected but no one would say at first was that it could be something far more profound. It was possible that Johnny had the brain chemistry of a person with schizophrenia. Although not strictly a hereditary disease, the disorder does seem to run in families. I never heard that uttered out loud in those first months of speculation.

Even though I had my suspicions, I was sympathetic to the notion that Johnny wasn't really that sick. He had always been a quiet kid, so his behavior didn't seem that strange to me. He was such a good student that teachers were often a little disappointed in me by comparison. More than once, I was encouraged to be more like him. It wasn't that I wasn't bright. I was but I was not anything like a model student. In our church youth group, he was equally well liked. He had grown into a tall, extremely handsome young man. He was athletic and well built, his glossy black hair swept to one side. Girls in the grade ahead of me befriended me to ask me about him. Everyone outside our family seemed to wonder what was wrong with *us* that we had a problem with *him*. It made me wonder if they were right. Why did we think Johnny was so strange?

All of us were experiencing the ambiguity of mental illness. People outside of our family saw the banal exterior of his disease, which easily passed for normal if you didn't look too closely. In closer quarters, Johnny was undeniably, though not unrelentingly, strange. In between all that typical teenager behavior, there was something off about the kid. He had an odd way of holding his face sometimes that made him seem like an empty shell. We learned to call this flat affect. He had peculiar ideas sometimes, inferences and beliefs that didn't seem to add up. We learned to call these delusions. Before I had language for it, all I had was the intuition that he wasn't experiencing the world quite the way I was.

I inferred this from a hundred small interactions, most of which I can't even recall distinctly. They added up to a sense that he was sick. These are the experiences that came to mind when I watched the scene between Donnie and Samantha Darko. Sometimes Johnny crept down the stairs three at a time, with his back against the wall. I asked him once why he did that. "It's like a game," he said. "It's so they don't hear me." I started to ask whom he meant but he disappeared into his room. I shook my head and laughed. In a week where he said nothing else out of the ordinary, it was easy to let it go.

On another day, I came into the kitchen to find Johnny putting a broken mug into the dishwasher. Again, his explanation was hazy. "I broke this," he said, "but it needs to be clean before I take it outside." I told him to put it in the trash right now. It doesn't need to be clean. He looked sheepish as he dropped it into he kitchen trash. He asked me not to say anything to anyone. Thinking he didn't want to get into trouble, I didn't.

It felt strange to be offering him that kind of advice when I was fourteen and he was nearly seventeen. He seemed in many ways much younger than me. I fancied myself mature for my age—I'm almost certain I wasn't—but it still felt peculiar. Besides that, anybody could break a mug.

As easily as I overlooked some interactions, others were harder to ignore. One day I came into the kitchen to find him putting masking tape on the sides of a cake pan. He started to giggle when he saw me, another odd habit he'd developed that made him seem younger than he was. He seemed profoundly embarrassed when I asked him what on earth he was doing.

"If I don't put tape on it," he explained, "then the batter will leak out." I didn't see any batter anywhere and I started to ask what he was trying to bake but pulled up short. That's when he showed me two evenly spaced punctures in either side of the pan. There was a kitchen knife beside him on the counter. I looked from the knife to Johnny and our eyes locked. He giggled and I laughed, too, even though I knew it wasn't funny. I told him he was about to start a fire in the oven. He threw the pan away and he asked me again not to tell anybody.

I didn't tell anyone about what I saw, at least not until much later. But I couldn't shake the fear that shot through me when I saw the knife. What he was doing with the knife didn't make any sense. He couldn't even explain rationally what he was doing with it. Even if he didn't intend to injure anybody with the knife, he was in danger of starting a fire in the oven. I went to sleep that night wondering what else he might do, counting out how many ways he could injure one of us. I wasn't yet worried that his rage would spill over into violence. He wasn't volatile by that point. But his thinking was clearly so bizarre, I worried he could injure someone without even realizing what he was doing.

Johnny's diagnosis of undifferentiated schizophrenia was a relief. As is often the case in these situations, we were happy to know what was wrong with him. The unknown is usually more terrifying than the truth and that was the case here. And given Johnny's mother's illness, it wasn't at all a surprise. A diagnosis brought the promise of treatment and a new hope that things could improve.

My relief was also about me. My own perception that Johnny was somehow ill was vindicated. All of those conversations that seemed strange really were strange. Everything that was uncertain or ambiguous about those exchanges seemed sure again. More bluntly, the diagnosis relieved my anxiety about my own mind. Karen Armstrong describes a similar relief about the soundness of her own mind, which came after she was diagnosed with epilepsy. She writes:

> For the first time in years, I felt that I could trust my perceptions. I knew now that my mind was neither broken nor irretrievably flawed. I was not mad, and need not expect to end my days in a locked ward. The world had been given back to me, and perhaps for the first time ever, I felt that I could take charge of my life.[7]

Diagnosis redefined symptoms that had been previously interpreted as signs of a deficient character. This empowered Armstrong, which is the sensation she describes here. In a strange way, this is exactly how I felt. If

---

7. Armstrong, *Spiral Staircase*, 182.

Johnny was sick, it meant that my mind was sound. His perception of the world was faulty and mine was not.

Johnny's diagnosis came on the heels of a major visual hallucination that my mother and I were both home to observe. Johnny was living in a studio apartment over our detached garage. The studio had vaulted ceilings with large windows near the roofline. The windows were uncovered. A person couldn't see into the living space through them and they let in ample natural light. Johnny hadn't turned off his lights at night for days, something my mother—a psychiatric nurse—had noticed with concern because insomnia can precede a psychotic break.

It was late morning and I was still in bed when I heard my mother arguing with Johnny. He was pacing back and forth between the house and the apartment. He was distraught, almost frantic. My mother was as keyed up as I'd seen her in a long time. They argued as she tried to get a straight answer out of him. She came into my room and demanded to know if I'd heard anything. Her anxiety alarmed me. She demanded again to know if I'd heard a car come up the driveway. When I said I hadn't, she told me to get dressed and come upstairs.

The house sat on seven acres out away from town, on a county road that wasn't even paved at the time. Behind the house, the woods sloped upward to the crest of the hill, where our property ended and gave way to a grass farm. The driveway itself was also unpaved. It wound through the trees up toward the house. We never saw more than a handful of cars in a given day and there was absolutely no reason for anyone to come up the driveway if they weren't there to visit us. Between tires on gravel and the dog, nobody could have made it up that driveway without someone knowing about it.

As implausible as the story sounded, my mother was clearly worried. When I came upstairs, she was asking Johnny a long series of questions in a repeating loop. Johnny looked positively miserable, like a chastened puppy. He gave the same answers every time. He saw a man in the driveway. He didn't hear him drive up. The man was short and he was wearing an orange vest like a road construction worker. None of this made any sense and she kept pressing.

"Where was he standing?"

"In the driveway."

"What was he doing? "

"He was looking at me." Johnny whispered it, his voice querulous. He seemed somewhere between confused and embarrassed. I pitied him intensely. He hesitated as if trying to remember something but he didn't say any more.

"Was it someone who was working on something? A meter reader, maybe?"

"I don't know."

"You know what they look like, don't you? Did he come up to the house?"

"No."

"Did he drive up in a car?"

"I didn't see."

"Did you hear a car?"

"I don't know."

"Did you hear a car?" she turned to ask me. Of course, I hadn't. She collected herself and he stood there, ears folded back and tail between his legs.

I couldn't say how long this went on but it felt like a very long time. Eventually my mother took a deep breath and regrouped. Johnny was tall enough that he could stand on tiptoes and peer out of the windows in the apartment but he must have had a reason to do that. She wanted to know what prompted him to look out the window if he didn't hear a car. This turned out to be the key.

"I saw his face looking in my window," Johnny said flatly. My mother stopped cold. Johnny could stretch to see out the windows of his apartment but for a person outside in the driveway to look into the windows was physically impossible. Johnny's claim that he saw a man's face in his window was about as unlikely as if he had said he saw a flock of squirrels sailing past the window in a tiny hot air balloon. It could not have been.

My mother released Johnny, who scurried out the back door to his apartment, and for a long time she didn't say anything. She sat with her chin on her hand and stared at the countertop—the same countertop, I remembered, where I'd found Johnny with the knife and cake pan. "The dog was asleep," she said finally. "When I came outside to find out what was wrong with Johnny, I stepped over the dog." We both weighed the gravity of this apparently mundane information. The dog dozed in the sun the entire time because there wasn't any car or man in an orange vest. The whole thing was a hallucination. None of it happened.

I've hallucinated just once. I had taken a cold medicine with a sleep aid in it. It's the sort of medicine they use to make methamphetamine.

I bought it by mistake but I decided to try it because I had a cold and couldn't sleep. I felt groggy and hungover the entire next day. I was sitting on my couch, unable to do much of anything but surf the Web. It was a Saturday and my husband had taken our daughter to the park. I was waiting for them to come home when I heard the car pull into the carport and the car door slam. Then I heard my daughter's voice: "Mommy! Come out here, we're home!" She sounded terrified so I rushed to the window to see if anything was wrong. No one was there.

I never took the pills again.

What stays with me is the terrified, lost feeling I had the moment I realized the voice wasn't real. Hearing her voice without being able to find her disoriented me. I couldn't remember where she was right away and I wandered through the rooms of our apartment to look for her. The feeling didn't entirely recede until my husband returned from the park for real and she was home again. Gradually, the world felt substantial again and I felt grounded again. The fear stayed with me until the next morning.

Johnny seemed equally lost the day he saw the man in the orange vest. After that day, he admitted that there were other hallucinations, mostly auditory. Don Mattingly used to chat with Johnny from the poster on the bedroom wall. There were other stories of voices chanting or telling him he loved Satan. These were neurological phenomena that lasted only moments. But if a three-second hallucination of my daughter's voice managed to unsettle me so seriously, I can only imagine the anguish recurring hallucinations would cause in a teenage boy.

It wasn't until many years later that Johnny first became homeless. He held jobs on and off but inevitably he quit or was fired. He lived with roommates for a while but they found him strange and creepy—I couldn't say I blamed them. We didn't see him very much anymore. We took him to dinner sometimes. Time apart made him seem even more strange. His conversations were disjointed. He seemed almost wholly uninterested in connecting with us. He spoke to us like we were all strangers with whom he had little or no relationship. I remember one dinner out when he made a strange series of comments about Colgate College. Another time, he was so upset by a movie we'd seen that he threw up in his mouth in the car. He didn't tell anyone but held it there, answering our questions with grunts until he could spit it out in the bushes by his front door. He seemed to make progress and then sabotage himself. Intelligent as ever, he was working toward a college degree but never finished. He couldn't (or wouldn't) hold a job for long. He went from living with roommates to living on his own and then to a group home. In the group home, he went off his medication and ended up living on the streets.

Like so many people with schizophrenia, he prefers not to take his medication. He rebels against the staid routine of the group home. He dislikes the inhibition of his freedom. I can't say that I blame him for any of that. As he has gotten older, his symptoms have become worse. He is increasingly volatile. He is still a well-built man and capable of doing some real damage.

Some years ago, my grandmother called me to tell me she saw him on the news in my hometown. I was living in another state but she thought I'd want to know. He left his group home after going off his medication and the police were looking for him. They were not looking for him to protect him. They were looking for him to protect the community from him. Time on the street seems to have hardened his self-protective instincts. He isn't paranoid as part of his disease but he is ready to defend himself. I later found the story in a local newspaper. As he left, he told the staff at the group home he was going to "ride the lightning on out of there." No one knew what that meant. When my grandmother called, she told me they said he was dangerous and shouldn't be approached. I went to sleep that night afraid of the things he might do.

Where Did You Sleep Last Night?

Leslie was enjoying his party thoroughly. Just after I arrived, he took the stage and rambled into the microphone about his favorite Westerns. He paused to tell a joke worthy of a drag queen: "Henry Fonda and I have a lot in common. He's Henry Fonda and I'm fond of Henry." The crowd laughed. After a few minutes, someone led him off the stage and the crowd applauded. They were staid but appreciative. Leslie danced in front of the stage as Toni Price performed, a kind of lurching jig. The crowd smiled but no one joined him. He made his way to the stage again and interfered with the performance. Price is a consummate professional and handled the intrusion with grace until someone came to lead Leslie off the stage. Banned from stage, he circulated through the crowd instead, thanking people for coming and posing for pictures. In each photo, he turned his backside to the camera and lifted his skirt to reveal his trademark thong.

There are times in life when you find yourself standing in the middle of a party drinking a cheap beer and plucking up the courage to introduce yourself to a homeless man in a zebra-print skirt. Or at least there are those times in my life. I didn't know anyone at the party. Except for the rather grand welcome he'd given me when I first arrived, I'd never met Leslie. We'd never talked. We were not even friends, as people seemed to assume when I told them I was writing about Leslie. I wasn't even particularly an expert on Leslie lore. I was just some woman standing nervously to one side watching everyone. When I did finally introduce myself to Leslie, I told him who I was, that I was writing about the homeless, and that I intended to write a chapter about him. He shook my hand and then leaned in to tell me something. I leaned forward to meet him and he said, "Do you know when it's okay for me to go on stage again?"

This is the awkward truth about my first and only meeting with Leslie Cochran. I don't know anything about him that I haven't gleaned from talking to people or reading their stories about him. Taken collectively, the stories I've heard about Leslie express a general ambivalence about the man. I don't mean ambivalence here primarily as a lack of certainty. I think people are pretty sure what they think about him. It's just that they don't think one thing all the time. Leslie is complicated and people project their own complexities onto his story. The sum is that people have strong negative and positive reactions to him. Even the people who most love and support him are pulled in multiple directions when it comes to Leslie.

Austin is a symbol of a life lived authentically and creatively, entirely outside of social norms. This is the primary reason Leslie is so beloved. If Austin were a religion, originality would be it's chief virtue. And Leslie is the patron saint of weird, especially among those who understand his homelessness as a choice rather than an unfortunate circumstance.

But if originality is a virtue, there's nothing worse than being a poser and this is where Leslie's public persona gets a bit complicated. I once brought up my adventures with the homeless at a kid's birthday party and the subject, as usual, turned immediately to Leslie. Once we'd all extolled the virtues of Leslie's outside-the-norm lifestyle and everyone had made the obligatory noises about valuing freedom and choice over social norms, someone brought up the rumor that Leslie owns a house in Tarrytown, one of Austin's most upscale neighborhoods. The rumor undermines Leslie's authenticity. If he's only pretending to be homeless, that isn't half as genuine as really being homeless. He would seem to lack the courage of his convictions if his performance of homelessness were only part-time. Of course, someone else suggested, it takes real chutzpah to pretend to be a homeless transvestite when you're really a homeowner. Even with that caveat, everyone concluded that it was wrong somehow for Leslie to earn enough money to buy a home in one of Austin's most expensive and exclusive neighborhoods by pretending to be something he wasn't.

People seem to enjoy unmasking Leslie as a fraud. They find a kind of cynical satisfaction in revealing something so Austin original as a fake. These are the same people who like to point out that "Keep Austin Weird" is a corporate slogan these days and not a counter-cultural rallying cry. The idea of Austin's most famous homeless person enjoying the fruits of his labor in a high-end home in a neighborhood none of us working stiffs could afford smacks of a delicious irony.

I couldn't say if there's any truth to the rumor that Leslie has a house but the story seems to serve at least two distinct functions. In the first place, it reassures people whose lives are at odds with their ideals. Maybe it's okay if underneath it all I still shop at Target and take my kids to soccer in a minivan. If Leslie is still Leslie in a West Austin house, maybe I'm okay, too. In the second place, it relieves an unspoken guilt. We all enjoy Leslie but we don't necessarily reward him for his performance. There are those who argue we have some responsibility to him—if you get your picture taken with him or you laugh at his jokes, you owe him some money. There are others who like to hope that he does all right whether or not they personally support him. Because if not we're all caught up in some kind of *schadenfreude*. We've projected our unfulfilled desire for an authentic and creative life onto a homeless guy and turned him into an icon of what we want. That seems less reprehensible if he isn't suffering. In other words, we feel better about professing how much we love Leslie if we aren't letting him sleep on the ground at night.

Chances are good that we are letting him sleep on the ground at night and this is where the issue becomes even more complicated. Everyone wants to help Leslie but the options are somewhat limited. We can give him money but we can't really dictate what he's going to do with that money. You could invite him to your house but then you'd have Leslie on your couch, doing things you'd rather he wouldn't do and refusing to stop. Helping him would likely mean changing some really fundamental things about him. Hiring managers generally aren't looking for an unwashed 60-year-old man in boobs and a skirt. Somehow the idea of Leslie owning a house is less outlandish than the idea of Leslie keeping a straight job for any length of time. He's too uncooperative and too flaky for that. Changing that would mean changing who he is and that isn't something that could or should be forced. I don't think Leslie wants to change and even if I thought he should, he's a grown adult. At some point it's absolutely none of my business if he sleeps on the ground at night.

As it happens, this is exactly the conundrum my family has when it comes to Johnny. Moving Johnny out of our house seemed like the only real option. It's remarkably difficult to maintain anything like a normal emotional connection with a schizophrenic person. His detachment from us is disturbing. Together with his tendency toward delusional thinking, it's not clear that he's a safe person to have sleeping in the next bedroom. He's easily overstimulated, so bringing him home for Thanksgiving dinner or the like isn't even an option. We never intended to abandon him to the care of mental health professionals but we didn't have the skills or resources to do otherwise. Johnny would probably rather not live in his group home. He has at times chosen to live on the streets as an alternative. But this is dangerous, both for him and for the community. Living on the streets puts an immense strain on an individual's physical health. The homeless are vulnerable to violence, both from one another and from those who target them. And in Johnny's case, he's a likely danger to others. Life on the streets is an unacceptable option. But the line between protecting him and the community and denying his right to direct his own life is dangerously thin. It may be for the best but it's hard not to feel like he's been incarcerated without committing a crime.

THE SKELETON IN THE CLOSET

The ambivalence I felt about Johnny's situation and his illness had an enormous effect on my intellectual life. Most of my early papers in college were about mental illness or homelessness. Later work branched into other areas but with a continued sensitivity to the fragility of the human psyche and the extreme complexity of social problems like poverty. These ideas have a straightforward connection with mental illness and Johnny's later homelessness. But I also wrote poetry and short stories about people losing their grip on reality. This wasn't always a bad thing in the worlds I created. Sometimes losing one world meant finding a different one. Science fiction and fantasy presented worlds completely different from my own and the possibility that things could be otherwise than they are. Later I was attracted to supernatural horror and the possibility of an uncanny world existing as the shadow side of this one. I even wrote a master's thesis on vampire stories as parallel shadow versions of stories about saints.

In hindsight, I understand all of these things as modes of working out a fundamental ambivalence in my experience of Johnny's illness. The intuition that an alternative to the world I experience exists grew out of knowing that Johnny didn't see the world the way I did. This other reality seemed at once fascinating and terrifying, both a safe realization and a frightening possibility. I vacillated between acknowledging that he was sick and believing that his reality was just as valid as my own. I reasoned that I could not determine that what Johnny experienced was any more or less real than the things I experienced. Fear kept me from fully embracing that position and all of its implications. On the one hand, I argued with myself that Johnny was just different and should be allowed to do whatever he wanted, including staying off his medication. But at night when I was alone and my fears crept in, I wanted nothing more than to know he was locked up somewhere.

In front of my mirror trying to decide on earrings for Leslie's party, I experienced these old anxieties and this deep-seated ambivalence. No one who really knows me is surprised to find me writing about a homeless transvestite. No one found it odd that I would turn up at his birthday party. I walk around on the edges of normal and generally do things my own way. What's less apparent is that I hang around the margins because the people who live at the margins scare me a little bit. And the best way I know to the handle things that scare me is to live with them. As a child, I developed a kind of phobia about skeletons after a neighborhood boy barricaded me in a closet with a glow-in-the-dark skeleton for a few moments. I had a recurring nightmare that involved a skeleton, a tolling bell, and Cap'n Crunch for months, until I made the skeleton into my imaginary friend. After that, he wasn't scary anymore.

Making friends with the skeleton is one of my ways of being in the world. Addressing my internal reaction to the homeless is an extension of that. It's both a way of making friends again with Johnny, at least in my heart and mind, and a way of coming to terms with the brokenness of our relationship. I see the same brokenness in Austin's complicated relationship with Leslie, and I recognize it in my own approach to the homeless in Austin. More than anything, I see a wound inside of me that produces an unsatisfactory reaction to all of these—Johnny, Leslie, and the homeless in general—that I call sin. It's all part of something that started a long time ago.

chapter three
Stevie Ray Hobo

Abba, give me a word.

Abba Xanthias said, "A dog is better than I am for he has love
and he does not judge."[1]

O NCE ON AN OTHERWISE ordinary afternoon, I met a man. I was
on my way home from teaching. It was late afternoon or early
evening. There was an unruly passenger on the bus that day, so
I got off downtown to wait for a transfer to another line. I walked to a
bus stop near the corner of Third and Congress to wait. I sat down on the
bench next to a worn-looking woman in white orthopedic shoes. I gave
her a quick smile and she nodded in reply.

We both turned to watching a hobo—I use the term because that's
what he called himself—on the corner. He was wearing a ragged leather
jacket, mid-calf length, and he had a straw cowboy hat perched on top of
his greasy head.

"Look at the hobo," he growled.

Stevie Ray Hobo, I thought.

He was spinning and shouting, "Wooo! Austin! I am going *off.*"
Someone on the opposite corner called to him but I couldn't hear what
was said. He shouted a reply: "My guitar's out of hock! I am going *off!*"
When he said guitar he pronounced it GEE-tar. The battered instrument
was slung across his back.

I sat there for a minute somewhere between enjoyment and concern.
His joy was infectious and I enjoyed that. He was also nattering like a
wild man, on the other hand, and that had me concerned. His appearance
was no wilder than the average urban camper but his behavior was truly
exceptional. He flung his arms out as he shouted and danced. Then he

1. *Sayings*, 159.

33

turned on his heel and faced me, his eyes glassy when I caught his gaze. I leaned down Congress to check for the bus.

Stevie Ray Hobo came toward the bench and spoke to us. He muttered something I couldn't understand to the woman, who took immediate offense. "I don't do no drugs! You get away from me, now," she commanded. She was a slight woman but her voice was forceful and domineering. He shrank back. "Aww, c'mon now. I was kidding. I don't do drugs either. At all. I mean," he looked at me slyly, "not today anyway." He laughed at his own joke and moved back to his corner.

Before I could react, a police car pulled into the intersection, made a U-turn, and stopped by the curb. A baby-faced officer with dark hair stepped out. I couldn't say who called him but the cop stepped out of his vehicle ready for a confrontation. They were too far away for us to hear the officer's replies.

"Awww, man," the hobo protested, "I didn't do nothing." And then, "I ain't got no drugs, I'm telling ya." After that, "No sirree, not me. I'm high on life." Stevie Ray Hobo laughed hard at that—so hard I laughed, too. That caught his attention and he came toward me. My heart started to pound.

"You believe me, right?"

"Sure," I told him. I wasn't sure if I did or didn't.

"I don't even do drugs," he said. After a pause, he added, "Most of the time." He waited for my response. I laughed again at that and he laughed, too. The police officer was still hovering.

"I'm going," he said over his shoulder. "You know, I got a right to be here. I wasn't doing nothing."

"You were bothering people," the cop shot back. "Move it out."

The hobo turned back to me. "You know," he added conspiratorially, "Willie Nelson got in trouble with the law, too." He paused thoughtfully. "I'm a little bit like him. I got my guitar."

"Don't you bother these ladies," the cop reiterated.

I was uneasy about being included in a complaint I didn't make. I wanted him to leave, though, so I didn't make a sound. I just watched. I looked down Congress again to see if the bus was coming. It wasn't. A red sports car pulled up to the stoplight. It was a warm spring day and the driver had the convertible top down. A dog sat on the passenger seat, panting. Stevie Ray Hobo glanced around before he slipped over.

"Hey! Can you smell that? Smell the hobo!" He spoke directly to the dog, who was already deeply involved in investigating Stevie Ray's coat sleeve. "Yeah, you can smell me a block away, can't ya?" He chuckled and then spun on his heel to face me.

"You see that?" He pointed to the dog.

"Yeah." I hesitated. I wasn't sure where this was going.

"He's sitting in that seat like he's a person."

"Yeah." Now I saw.

"That's the world for you. A dog gets treated like a person . . ." He trailed off with a quick look around to see who was listening.

"You get it?" he asked me.

"I get it," I said. And I did.

chapter four
Sin

Abba, give me a word.

Abba Alonius said, "If I had not destroyed myself completely, I should not have been able to rebuild and shape myself again."[1]

IF I ACCEPT WHAT I've always been told about myself, my greatest spiritual fault is that I think too much. I have been told this many times by many different people. Growing up in conservative evangelical churches, I heard again and again that faith should be about your heart and not your head. I was smart and serious as a teenager, bookish and interested in what probably seemed like obscure theological questions. Whatever trouble I had, I was usually diagnosed with too much head and not enough heart.

As far as anybody could tell me, the cure for this was for me to become a different person from the one I am. This didn't sit well. My way of approaching life wasn't quite like everyone else. But if Jesus made me this way, why should I change it? That was my question and for a long time, no one could answer it for me.

Too much thinking has never really been my problem and in the end, I rejected the very idea of a split between thinking and feeling. I feel my intellectual commitments deeply. I wouldn't have made teaching and writing about spirituality my life's work if I didn't. Sorting out the intellectual content of a theology is hard emotional work. It's less about tossing around a few ideas and more a matter of bringing to the surface what we know (or think we know) about God—that knowledge that sits in our bones at the core of who we really are. It hurts. You're a bundle of raw spiritual nerves and everybody is on them. And when it's all on the surface, you're not done. Beliefs have to be sifted and shifted. I often hear people call

1. *Sayings*, 35.

36

seminary training intellectual and dry, heady rather than hearty. I think there might be less crying and fighting in seminary if that were true.

By now when someone tells me I'm too much in my head, I tell them I feel with my brain and think with my heart. The idea that there is a split between the head and the heart is actually thoroughly modern, and the fact that the desert fathers and mothers lack any such framework is part of what attracted me them in the first place. They might not have encouraged my educational pursuits but I don't think they would have concluded easily that my big problem was too much thinking.

That doesn't mean I'm off the hook. It doesn't even mean that all those times I was accused of too much thinking I wasn't doing something wrong. Not long ago, I found an old journal I wrote when I was about seventeen years old. In it, I complain at some length about my Bible study group. It wasn't as rigorous as I wanted. The leaders weren't as sharp. They weren't correcting people when I thought they should. They weren't teaching me anything new. It just wasn't enough and I wasn't satisfied pursuing knowledge on my own. I wanted the whole group running with a bit more fervor and intellectual precision. When I complained, I was reminded that not everybody was as smart as me. If I pressed, they told me I had to get out of my head.

The journal records my frustration. I wanted a faith with real intellectual depth. This is not in itself a bad thing. But wanting the group to run according to my agenda wasn't the best thing, nor was hearing that I was particularly smart a good thing because it made me feel like I was different. I vacillated between thinking the group should run to suit my interests because I was somehow uniquely equipped to determine our course and thinking I should quit the group altogether because I wasn't right for it. Again, I didn't think I was superior necessarily. I did think I was a special case—something that made me feel superior some of the time and inferior the rest of the time.

The truth is that I wasn't different. I was locked in a struggle against my own pride. I am tempted to focus my attention on the ways I see pride at work in others. This relieves my anxiety about my own pride and it soothes my ego. This temptation is strongest with respect to my own particular areas of failing. And so it follows that I am sorely tempted to write a story about the way our culture or society ignores or dismisses the homeless. And it might be a true story. It would still be a deflection from the hard truth in front of me. I am broken. I am unkind. I ignore the suffering of others. And I do this because I am comfortable, relatively wealthy, and self-assured.

This is where I meet the Abbas and Ammas and they expose the heart of sin: not my brokenness so much as the pride that refuses to acknowledge it. Pride feeds sin because it hides sin—from my own eyes, at least—so that my brokenness cannot be healed. If this is a story about sin, I mean sin in a very ordinary sense. I mean the daily condition of my interior life—that way of being that is always with me, as it is with all human beings. It is the reason I fail, again and in new and surprising ways, to recognize my fellow human beings as creatures in the image of God. Pride shields me from my failures and spares my ego but it does so at the expense of my soul. If I can't acknowledge the ways I fail, I can't root out their causes. If I can't do that, I can't participate with the Holy Spirit in my own healing. The truth stripped of pride is simply this: I am a sinner. And unless I acknowledge that I fail, I can't even begin to cultivate virtue.

ABBA, WHAT MUST I DO TO BE SAVED?

The desert fathers and mothers took it for granted that humility was the most powerful of all the virtues. A saying associated with Amma Theodora relates the story of an anchorite who had tremendous power over demons. He asked the demons why they fled from him so readily and they answered back. What good is fasting against a being that neither eats nor drinks? And what good is an all-night vigil against a being that has no need for sleep? Even separation from the world, the cornerstone of monastic life, is no use. If you go to the desert, the demons are there, too. Finally, the demons admit that the only thing that affects them is humility. Amma Theodora's conclusion is that pursuing humility is primary. The trappings of asceticism, whether fasting, vigils, or separation from the world, are secondary.[2] The practices are only useful if they cultivate humility.

This is an important point to remember for those who practice them. They are not ends in themselves, for a start. Not only that but it's very easy for ascetic practice to become a point of comparison, and after that, a point of pride. The intent of Amma Theodora's statement is to remind her audience of this simple fact. Christian practice must never interfere with humility because without humility, we have nothing.

2. Ibid., 84.

Humility isn't the most popular virtue these days, in conversation or in practice. When I teach theology to college-age students, they are less excited about the idea of humility as a core Christian virtue than they are about the possibility of liberation or the prophetic call for justice. They prefer the idea of an active faith that raises its voice to one that is focused on interior life. Their preferred mode of faithfulness more closely resembles the spirit of the civil rights movement than contemplation. Humility, as far as most of them can see, is less important than righteous indignation.

The wisdom of the desert moves in the opposite direction. Calling for justice requires a self-assurance that is contrary to the humility proposed by the desert fathers and mothers . You can't call another person to justice unless you are absolutely sure you are in the right—that is to say, you must be sure you know what justice is and be able to name it simply for every situation. Knowing what is right is easy enough. Calling out the sins of another is not. Although they were hardly situational ethicists, the Abbas and Ammas look to God for justice rather than enforcing it themselves. In a story about Abba Agathon, the old man is asked a question about lying. His reply infers that lying itself is not the problem. He illustrates by telling a story:

> Suppose two men have committed a murder before your eyes and one of them fled to your cell. The magistrate, seeking him, asks you, "Have you seen the murderer?" If you do not lie, you will deliver that man to death. It is better for you to abandon him unconditionally to God, for he knows all things.[3]

It isn't that lying is good. It is a sin, without question. Murder is also a sin. There is no question of that. There is also no question in this hypothetical situation that the man is guilty. But to deliver a man to his death amounts to another murder. He may deserve death but it isn't necessarily our place to carry out the punishment. As with many of the sayings, this is a conundrum that is meant to drive home a point. It is intended at some level to offend the sensibilities of the listener. The Abba isn't making a prescription about what we should do in every case, but the story does illustrate the radical nature of the Gospel. The murderer's guilt doesn't mean we have power over his life. It is still better to abandon the guilty man unconditionally to God's mercy.

3. Ibid., 35.

There are two principles beneath this. The first is an ethic of compassion over righteousness. There is a story about Abba Ammonas and a young woman pregnant out of wedlock that illustrates. The local people brought the young woman to him and asked him to give her a penance. As the local holy man, he was in a position of authority. Everyone present would have accepted his judgment, likely including the young woman. But instead of punishing her, he made the sign of the cross on her pregnant belly and provided her with sheets of linen. This was an act of kindness. If she didn't survive childbirth, the linens could be used as a shroud for her and the child, so they could have a proper burial. Those who accused her were furious and demanded that he punish her. His reply was simple: "Look, brothers, she is near to death; what am I to do?"[4]

The gathered crowd wasn't expecting this reaction and they were surely right that Abba Ammonas should consider the woman a sinner—and perhaps even a very grave sinner. It is all but certain that he would have but he didn't react to her as a just man passing judgment on someone less worthy. Rather than holding his own righteousness over her head, he approached her as Christ would have and had compassion on her distress. If her actions were sinful, she was bearing the consequences—a woman destitute, on the point of death, and facing down an incredible ordeal. The fact that she was also a sinner is as incidental as noting that she is also a human being.

The story exemplifies the Abba's ethic of compassion over righteousness. In some sense, he had every right to pass judgment on her and yet he didn't. From his own perspective, I'm sure he didn't think he had the right. His only duty was to respond to her in love. This act of mercy had some effect on the bystanders—we are told that they never dared to bring anyone else before him that way again—and we can hope they understood the lesson.

This relates to the second principle behind these stories. A man like Abba Ammonas embraced the real equivalence of sins. Abba Theodore gives this advice: "If you are temperate do not judge the fornicator, for you would then transgress the law just as much. And he who said, 'Do not commit fornication,' also said, 'Do not judge.'"[5] Whatever the sins of another person, they are not more grave than your own.

4. Ibid., 27.
5. Ibid., 80.

It follows that the desert fathers and mothers would find something amiss in a call for justice that was not both tempered by compassion and inward looking. Sin is pervasive in every human life, which means we can always find sins in other people to criticize. But sin is always met with redounding divine compassion. Every sin arises from a broken place, a wound. Sin is always a sign that healing is needed. Cuts and bruises aren't improved by shouting. If compassion rules our dealings with the people around us, it frees the energy we need to look inward. With respect to justice, the first question is not, "How are *they* unjust?" The first (and last) question must be, "How am *I* unjust?" The next question must be, "What is broken in us that makes us so?" After that, we must take our medicine and exercise our sore joints. And of course, we must pray for health.

If our salvation is a change in status rather than a real change in the condition of our souls, then what I'm describing is unnecessary effort. Worse yet, it lends itself to self-righteousness. At the other end of the spectrum, I often hear the sentiment that our chief problem as Christians is that we're too hard on ourselves. I wonder how that could be further from the truth when we take shelter in our identity as good people and at the same time we eschew all effort as unnecessary to salvation.

There is a danger of self-righteousness and pride implicit in all of this. There is also a direct line between what I'm talking about as a mode of Christian living and a theology of the atonement. The spirituality embodied by the Abbas and Ammas suggests quite a different understanding of atonement than a standard penal substitutionary model. There is a climactic passage in the *Life of Anthony* in which Anthony emerges from the fortress where he has wrestled with temptation for years on end. He emerges fresh as a daisy, by Athanasius's account, which is something of a surprise to onlookers. This is understandable, given that they've been overhearing his struggle. Their awed reaction is paralleled by Athanasius's description of the man:

> The state of his soul was one of purity, for it was not constricted by grief, nor relaxed by pleasure, nor affected by either laughter or dejection. Moreover, when he saw the crowd, he was not annoyed any more than he was elated at being embraced by so many people. He maintained utter equilibrium, like one guided by reason and steadfast in that which accords with nature.[6]

6. Athanasius, *Life of Anthony*, 42.

Athanasius describes the state of Anthony's soul here as written on his face. He is neither worn down by grief nor overcome with the joy of the crowd. Rather, he exists in a state of perfect *apatheia*— literally freedom from passions. This is not apathy but rather the complete harmony of his faculties, reasonable and emotive. His *apatheia* means that his appetites and emotions are under the direction of his reason and thus nothing in his soul—and therefore in his body—is out of balance. He is like Adam before the Fall—as a human being should be. Looking to a nearer precedent, he is like Jesus, the New Adam.

The Abbas and Ammas might have resonated with the idea that salvation is about restoration or healing but their goal was never to write a theology. They weren't so much interested in giving an account of God as they were in experiencing God. What they learned was that it's impossible to make progress without effort. They knew that effort, although necessary, was not enough. It might lead to pride instead of humility—a situation that required a shift in thinking or perhaps in practice. Above all, they knew that prayer was the heart of their life and the true path to humility. Humility is a path that lies between the danger of self-hatred on one end, which denigrates the precious gift of human life given to us by God, and self-righteousness on the other, which stubbornly refuses to acknowledge that life is a gift. The middle way between these poles is self-accusation.

THE WAY OF SELF-ACCUSATION

The propensity to ruminate on the failings of other people is not new or special. It is perhaps the most thoroughly ordinary thing each of us can do. It's little surprise then that addressing this temptation is an integral part of the Christian monastic tradition. Few classes of people are more universally prone to self-righteousness than ascetics, who spend long hours accomplishing feats of fasting and prayer. In the era following Constantine's conversion, a steady stream of men and women fled to the Egyptian desert. They came to retreat from the world and to live lives wholly dedicated to God. They understood better than most the human tendency to focus on the sins of other people, which is really a matter of self-deception. If I focus on your sins, I can avoid dealing with mine. And since addressing one's own sinful nature is a central goal of asceticism, the impulse to focus outward instead of inward is especially destructive.

In order to curb this tendency, the desert fathers and mothers adopted a posture of perpetual self-accusation. The idea that self-accusation is in any way a good thing is somewhat counter-intuitive for modern people. The need for self-compassion is held up against the tendency of outside forces to impose harsh restrictions and judgments on the individual. Negative self-talk is recognized as destructive, and as it is rooted out, the practice of affirmation is inserted in its place. These are the tenets of our modern psychological framework. And there is a great deal of value in them.

Yet the desert fathers and mothers still have something to contribute and many of them understood self-accusation as the spiritual discipline most worth cultivating. These ancient men and women were working from a psychology that differs significantly from our own and yet, they, too, were human. And they recognized that comparison, to paraphrase a teacher I once had, is the cancer of the soul. In looking outward, we become so agitated that we shrivel and decrease. In looking inward, we find a peace that supports peculiar growth.

But when we look inward, we must strive to see with clear eyes. If we're honest with ourselves, what we see there is not all positive. Each and every one of us has negative qualities, bad habits, and ugly thoughts. Each and every one of us—again, if we are honest—has done things that were wrong. Some of these actions were mistakes and we realized the error only in hindsight. But we've all also chosen to do things that we knew were wrong—actions that harmed ourselves and harmed other people. It's the common heritage of humankind that this is true for all of us.

Honesty is the beginning of self-accusation as a way of deepening spiritual life, and yet peace, not despair, is ultimately its outcome. Abba John the Dwarf calls self-accusation a light burden. But rather than taking up this light burden—an allusion to the easy yoke of the gospel—we load ourselves with an even heavier burden, namely, self-justification.[7] There's a commonsense wisdom to this. I'm capable of expending a great deal of energy justifying my own bad behavior. There's a very real sense in which it would be easier—and thus a lighter burden—to simply admit fault. It is perhaps more painful to admit that I'm wrong if we're measuring the injury to my ego but it is not more difficult in terms of energy expended.

7. *Sayings*, 90.

Injury to ego is part of the goal of self-accusation, where ego is understood not as the true core of a person but rather as the false, justifying self that prevents us from seeing ourselves and others clearly. It is the ego that blinds and binds, even as it prevents us from humble, authentic life. The desert fathers and mothers understood this, too. Abba Alonius said, "If I had not destroyed myself completely, I should not have been able to rebuild and shape myself again."[8] There is something of ourselves that ought to be destroyed in order that something purer and truer can rise out of the ashes. The thought resonates with Buddhist wisdom as much as with Jungian psychology. To kill yourself in dreams is unnerving but, from a Jungian perspective, heralds new life. Without injuring your body, there is promise in the act of killing a former self in order to make way for something new. And self-accusation is integral to this process insofar as "not understanding what has happened prevents us from going on to something better," in the words of Abba Poeman.[9] Understanding well how I have failed prevents me from unconsciously repeating the same mistakes. Identifying the failures of my false self assists in the process of breaking down what needs to be dismantled, again in order to make way for something better.

The salutary effects of self-accusation counteract the harm done by self-righteousness. Abba Poeman's sayings encourage the listener to self-accusation as a way of attaining inner peace. In his words: "Let go of a small part of your righteousness and in a few days you will be at peace."[10] Paradoxically, it is self-righteousness that agitates us, not self-accusation. Self-righteousness cannot metabolize and account for our failures. If I am self-righteous, the things I've done and continue to do wrong violate my sense of self, which is rooted in a false sense of my own goodness. The same wrongdoings cannot stir up any panic if they are not a threat to my identity. In that sense, there is peace in admitting my failings to myself and to God.

The parallel temptation is to self-hatred. Self-righteousness is clearly rooted in pride. I am self-righteous if I am convinced that I am a special case somehow—more righteous, more spiritually advanced, and even less tempted to sin than others. If by self-justification I can avoid confronting

8. Ibid., 35.
9. Ibid., 200.
10. Ibid., 187.

my sin, I do not have to face the full, uncomfortable reality of who I am. Paradoxically, self-hatred is also at times an expression of pride. If I am convinced that I am a special case, more sinful than others, less worthy of mercy than the rest. This often manifests itself in both internal and external narratives of unworthiness, which can run in an obsessive loop in both thought and conversation. Like self-righteousness, this is a way of salving my interior discomfort with facing the truth about myself—including the truth that I am ultimately just like everyone else.

Self-accusation walks a path between self-righteousness and self-hatred. On the one hand, it eschews the temptation to believe that my sins are somehow not really sinful or that the sins of others are categorically worse. On the other, it keeps back from an obsessive self-hatred that would make my sinfulness especially offensive. It is rather the acknowledgment that I fail. There is a relevant saying from the desert:

> A brother said to Abba Poeman, "If I fall into a shameful sin, my conscience devours and accuses me saying: 'Why have you fallen?'"
> The old man said to him, "At the moment when a man goes astray, if he says, I have sinned, immediately the sin ceases."[11]

The brother's conscience engages in what looks like self-accusation to modern eyes. In the face of sin, he can only ask himself why, why have you fallen? There's a note of despair in this. After so much effort and so much time, how is it that I continue to fall and fail? Why have you, who have dedicated your life to holiness, fallen so mightily?

But this is not self-accusation. It is the dark underbelly of self-righteousness. When we build up a false sense of the self as righteous, as if we were somehow not prone to sin, we have nowhere to go but down. When we fail, this false identity shatters. What the brother experiences is the plunge from the artificial height of self-righteousness to the low realization that he is not truly righteous after all. The brother's conscience afflicts him with the question why, as if he ought to do better.

The story resonates with one of the few positive lessons Karen Armstrong took from her years as a Roman Catholic nun. She describes being asked about her feelings of guilt by a curious friend. She observes rightly that people often associate guilt with Catholicism. But while Armstrong grieves the failure of her spiritual life in the convent, what she feels is not guilt. She writes:

11. Ibid., 181.

> One of the good things that I had learned from my superiors was that guilt could be pure self-indulgence, a wallowing in the ego. Guilt, I was told, usually sprang from misplaced pride; it might simply be chagrin that you were not as wonderful as you hoped.[12]

Like Armstrong, I am sometimes asked about guilt. Most presume that an emphasis on personal failing necessarily produces guilt. Although I do not feel the kind of sadness she describes, what I am trying to describe is not an emotional experience. It is a practice.

Self-accusation undermines the mental process of guilt. Guilt has an emotional component but it can easily become habitual. Armstrong describes it as a form of self-indulgence. We may engage in the mental and verbal rehearsal of our faults. This kind of negative self-talk takes many forms and is especially common among women. Guilt might also manifest itself in an endless loop of rationalization for various behaviors. Self-accusation replaces the relentless wrangling of a conscience in turmoil. In place of guilty self-justification, self-accusation earnestly tries to acknowledge failures with clear eyes.

Self-righteousness is volatile because it is false and self-accusation is stable and salutary because it is true. The truth is simple. Of course I have sinned. I am a sinner. Although I struggle against it, it is within my condition to fail. Unlike self-righteousness, the truth of this identity is steady and stable. It is not threatened by failing and it is not threatened by virtue. Unlike self-righteousness, it can account for both realities.

The story about Abba Poeman quoted above suggests a straightforward way to discern the difference between honest assessment of self and self-justifying guilt. Guilt torments. It never releases its grip. It will not let us forget what we have done and that we should not have done it. To the contrary, when an honest assessment has been made the experience is over. Like dreams or visions, if a feeling of peace follows, then it is a holy impulse. If you feel worse afterwards, if the guilt keeps at you, it is not of God.

Self-accusation is the acknowledgment of sin, not as a cataclysmic event or an unforgivable crime but rather as a consistent failure to live the fullness of a human life. I fail. I begin again. I fail and I begin again. This is the truth about me. And self-accusation is the means by which I call to mind this truth and live this reality. It releases me from the need to maintain the illusion that it isn't true. It liberates me to start over. I fail

12. Armstrong, *Spiral Staircase*, 51.

and I begin again. As Abba Poeman said of Abba Pior, every day we make a new beginning.[13]

There is pain inherent in this process. It is painful and it takes a commitment to constant work to maintain awareness of one's sins and to keep the ego from rebuilding its self-justifications. It is not for nothing the Abbas and Ammas sometimes call it a burden. But it is not a heavy burden. It is freedom. There is real wisdom in acknowledging that destruction is a creative process. When one thing is destroyed, something new can arise. As my self-righteousness dies, a freer woman emerges, more loving and compassionate, more able to bear life's difficulties patiently. Taking myself apart hurts but it's worth every ounce of effort. Every day a new beginning.

13. *Sayings*, 179.

chapter five
The Smell of Death

Abba, give me a word.

Abba Agathon said, "If I could meet a leper, give him my body and take his, I should be very happy. That indeed is perfect charity."[1]

ONE DAY I WAS on my way to class and the bus was particularly crowded. It was hot. When it's hot outside and the bus is crowded, that's when I notice the smell. They keep the 1L/1M buses very cold, which helps with the smell, but sometimes it isn't enough. I chose a seat toward the front of the bus, in the area reserved for the elderly and disabled. A woman boarded and sat down next to me. Immediately I was overcome by a strong odor of urine. She shifted in her seat and I realized she was wearing an adult diaper and it was soiled. The urine mixed with the smell of her body was enough to make me gag.

It's a smell I know all too well. Some days, it lingers in my clothes even after I leave the bus. The bus was full and men and women were standing in the aisles, so there was no question of changing seats. I thought for a moment about getting off to wait for the next bus. I didn't think I had time so I hunkered down, hand over my mouth, head and body turned away from her, and thought about the groundlings I remember from my days as an English major. The smell couldn't have been much worse than the un-washed masses on the ground in front of the stage in Shakespeare's Globe Theater. My Shakespeare instructor told us they sold oranges among the groundlings. The fresh citrus counteracted the general miasma of body odor. I have no idea if any of that is true but I couldn't help thinking about how it would work. I sat there with my head turned away from the source of the odor and thought, *my kingdom for an orange.*

1. *Sayings,* 24.

This is how I came to be sitting toward the front of the bus with my body angled toward the front door when a man got on and stood directly in my line of sight. He was homeless but relatively clean. He wore a plaid button-down shirt, long-sleeved, and jeans. None of this was remarkable. What made him memorable was the massive purple growth on his face. It was the color of a port wine stain, easily four inches long, a bulbous mass that stood out from his skin by several inches. I have never seen anything like it, before or since. It struck me at the time as the sort of thing you might see in a developing nation.

I wanted to look directly at it but I didn't want to stare. I wanted to see it but I didn't want to look too closely. I was drawn in and repulsed all at the same time. I couldn't turn my head away without turning toward the smell. I stole a look and caught the man's eye. He smiled and I'm sure he was fully aware of my discomfort. I smiled weakly back and let my eyes fall to the floor.

The man with the growth on his face struck up a conversation with someone, I don't recall, or maybe he was just talking. "A photographer took my picture," he announced proudly. No one responded. "Yeah, for an art show," he added. "Can you believe it?"

As a matter of fact, I could.

"He was real nice to me and everything."

I believed that, too. I wasn't sure if he was addressing someone specific, so I looked up and caught his eye. I smiled again and nodded slightly. He smiled back. I assumed that was the end of it and it would have been except a hipster-looking guy a few rows back decided to speak up.

The hipster had an artfully tousled crop of black hair and wore an Irish fisherman's cap, tight plaid pants, and suspenders. His face was set in a scowl. He didn't mince words. "Shut up already, you asshole. No one wants to hear what you're saying and no photographer took your picture anyway."

The homeless man seemed crestfallen for a moment and the air suddenly felt heavy and tense. Everyone waited for a response. The homeless man shifted his weight but seemed unperturbed. "Well, I'm sure sorry if you didn't want to hear it but a photographer did take my picture and that's the truth."

"Give it up, already. Who would want your picture?"

"A real-life photographer, I'm telling you. For an art show."

"Dude, think about it. Who wants to be in an art gallery and look up and see your ugly face. It's stupid so quit saying it."

I listened with interest. I couldn't think of a single reason to doubt the story about the photographer. The deformity was striking even if it didn't seem debilitating. There was the contrast between white skin and purple growth and the way it nearly enveloped one eye. I could easily imagine myself standing in a gallery transfixed. I also couldn't think of a single reason to dispute someone on the bus, even if it had been the most unbelievable lie. To do it in such ugly terms seemed even more inscrutable. This hip kid with his carefully cultivated cool had the demeanor of a playground bully.

I was on the point of saying something when someone else interjected. He turned to address the hipster directly. "Dude! No one cares what your stupid hipster ass has to say. If he says a dude took his picture, he took his picture."

Not to be silenced, the hipster shot back that there was no way this could be true. The two men fell to arguing. First they argued about whether the story was true. Then they argued about why, in the name of all things compassionate, anybody would pick on a homeless man. The hipster had no good answer to this and I wondered if he also kicked puppies in his spare time. Before long other passengers were encouraging both men to shut up already.

The man with the purple growth was harmless, even endearing, but the argument that erupted around him unnerved me, just as any argument in an enclosed public space might. None of it had anything to do with me and I never saw any of the people involved again. I felt drawn into the story. I took a side, mentally, but I didn't move. I said nothing and I kept my eyes on the floor because I was afraid. Between my fear and the smell, I thought seriously about getting off the bus. I heaved a sigh of relief when the hipster in the plaid pants abruptly got up and left.

The man with the growth on his face got off a few blocks later and when he left, I realized the woman sitting next to me was also gone. I didn't notice when she left. The smell hung in the air. I stepped off the bus at the corner of Congress and Oltorf and lifted my sleeve to my nose. It was still there, hanging on me like a disease I hoped I wouldn't catch.

chapter six
Overcoming Passion

Abba, give me a word.

Abba Poeman said, "I will have no mercy upon you, nor will God have any, if you yourself do not make an effort and if you do not pray to God."[1]

A NUMBER OF YEARS ago, I took a research trip to Greece. While I was there, I took a bus from Athens to Elefsina. I was with a friend and we had plans to visit the sanctuary of Demeter and Kore at Eleusis. On the way, we decided to stop at the monastery in Dafni. We got off a little too early and as we were walking, a dog joined us. Athens is overrun with stray dogs, so this was hardly surprising. In the city center, they're pretty docile and spend most of their time sleeping in the shade. Outside of town, they can be a little bit more aggressive. Loose dogs make me nervous and this one was following along behind us nipping at our heels, yapping, and generally making a nuisance of himself. We ignored him and when that didn't work, we tried to get rid of him. He wouldn't go away, so we made our peace and named him Triptolemos after one of the heroes of Eleusis. I was relieved when we finally got back on the bus and left him behind.

I tell this story because it's a kind of parallel to my behavior toward the homeless. They make me nervous. I do what I can to ignore them. If I can't ignore them, I try to run them off. If that doesn't work, I give them a disarming nickname—something like Stevie Ray Hobo—and breathe a sigh of relief when it's time for me to get on (or off) the bus and get away from them. Stevie Ray Hobo made the point that people treat him worse than a dog. I'm no different. As far as my behavior is concerned, he might as well have been a stray dog on the side of the highway outside of Athens.

Nicknames aren't my only distancing behavior. Just as often, I'm seized by an urge to jump off at the next stop. I don't always resist this

1. *Sayings,* 187.

urge. The last time it happened, I got off just before 34th Street, nearly ten blocks before my normal stop. I was sitting between two homeless men. The first sat by the window to my right. He had a Fanta bottle filled with what I'm sure was beer. He reeked of alcohol and his head wagged with the motion of the bus like he couldn't keep it steady. I sat down in the aisle seat next to him because the bus was crowded and it was an open space. He acknowledged me and I nodded. Across the aisle, the second man leered at me with a grin like a hyena. I concentrated on my book. The man across the aisle continued grinning at me. Now and then he laughed softly. The man next to me drank surreptitiously from his bottle and tried to keep his head steady.

After a while, I realized the man by the window was staring at me intently. When I couldn't ignore him anymore, I stole a quick look. He took the opportunity to speak. "Heeyyyy," he drawled. He was a diminutive Hispanic man and he spoke with a thick accent. "Yeah?" I replied. He asked, "Do you like have a phone?" I was holding my cell phone in my hand, so the question confused me at first. I asked him to repeat himself and then I held up a phone to show him that, yes, like any normal person I did have a phone. "That's good," he said. "You got like a number or something?" he asked and before I could reply, demanded, "Give it to me."

I thought the idea of a homeless guy with the chutzpah to demand my phone number was unbearably funny, so I laughed and he laughed and we were having such a good joke that the homeless guy across the aisle laughed, too. Then we stopped laughing and I realized he was waiting for an answer. I said no, I would not. He surprised me by insisting. His demeanor was friendly enough but his persistence was fierce. I tried to put him off by telling him I was married. "Oh," he exclaimed. From across the aisle, his friend said, "Too bad!" But then he changed tactics, "Okay, then. Just like for a friend or whatever." I pictured the two of us meeting for coffee and this sent me into a fresh wave of giggling. But of course I still told him no.

What I did next felt very urgent at the time but probably wasn't. He casually asked me if I was getting off soon and I didn't like the question. I didn't want him to know where I was getting off and I suddenly hoped he would get off before me so he wouldn't have the chance to follow me off the bus. It happened that, just as I had this thought, someone else requested a stop and when I saw the doors open, I bolted out of my seat and onto the pavement.

"This is your stop?" he called after me. Of course it wasn't. We weren't near any apartments or houses. Unless I lived in an office park or at the gas station, this was not my stop. But I bolted and I started walking like a maniac, looking over my shoulder every few seconds to see if I was being followed. Unsurprisingly, no one got off behind me. As I watched the bus disappear up the street, I considered my options. I could wait for the next bus. I could walk home. I could walk a few blocks around the corner and try to catch a different bus line.

Before I did anything, I called my husband to tell him I would be late. He wanted an explanation and I had to tell him a homeless man asked me for my phone number and I jumped off the bus ten blocks early in a panic. My husband, never one to pull any punches, told me that this was stupid.

It was stupid and it was completely typical of me. It's the reason that, after two years of riding the 1L/1M, I decided to change my route completely. For two years, I walked about half a mile to the bus stop and rode it straight to St. Edward's without making any transfers. It took just under an hour door to door and it was easy. After two years, I decided to make a change. I caught the 5 bus in front of my house and rode it downtown, changing buses at Congress and Cesar Chavez where I caught the 1L/1M and rode it the rest of the way to work.

Not coincidentally, this is the same attitude I took to Johnny after his diagnosis of schizophrenia. I did whatever I could to avoid him because he scared me. I did have some affection for Johnny. We played together as kids and that's a bond that isn't easily erased. I had already embraced a theology that prompted me to look for Christ in the least among us—the homeless, the stranger, and the prisoner. I had a bone to pick with Christians who didn't seem to think that helping the poor was commanded by Scripture. I also wanted him to move out of our house as soon as possible and I wasn't very much interested in where he went. My discomfort about Johnny's mental state trumped all of my higher ideals. I would have happily seen him institutionalized if it meant I didn't have to interact with him on a daily basis.

This is not a charming story but it's absolutely true. It's something I think we often face, this friction between our ideals and the reality of living those ideals. It's very nice to profess a deep love for humanity but when it comes to the daily chore of loving actual human beings, it gets a little bit tough. I still believe that loving the people we like least is exactly what we're called to do as Christians. That's ultimately why I'm telling this less than flattering story. It's evidence of my sin.

I could cover for myself. I could tell a story about how it's understandable and therefore okay that I have done these things. I have a right to protect myself. Besides that, maybe given my history it's just too difficult to stay in contact with the homeless, especially if they're mentally ill. Or maybe I could hide behind a sometimes homeless brother to establish my credibility as someone who supports the homeless. I could do all of that and some of it might be true. It would still be a cover. The cold fact is I avoid certain kinds of people even though they have never injured or even threatened me in any way. I avoid and distance myself from them as if they were objects rather than people. I have done this unthinkingly and all because encountering them moved me deep inside and I allowed those feelings to dictate my actions.

THE ANATOMY OF A PASSION

My use of the term *feeling* here is somewhat misleading. What I mean is something more like what the desert fathers and mothers would call a passion. Defined simply, a passion is a movement of the soul that overwhelms reason. Since the Abbas and Ammas understood that reason was closely allied with love, being overwhelmed by the passions causes us to act in ways that are contrary to the law of love. And any action that is contrary to love is, by definition, sinful. Passions are therefore an experience that precedes sin. They tempt us to sin. If we are not aware of them, they carry us into sin without our conscious awareness that we are in sin. A passion is not a sin but without the passions, we would all act out of love for God, self, and neighbor and there would be no sin.

This is most likely a counter-intuitive definition of passion for most modern readers. Passion has taken on a distinct connotation in modern vocabulary. At least since the Romantic movement, a passion has been conceived positively as "something like an intense emotion or a great commitment to something wonderful, if slightly bizarre."[2] One might have a passion for justice, or more comically, a passion for grapefruit. In this sense, God might be said to have a passion for justice or perhaps grapefruit. More pointedly, God is sometimes said to have a passion for us. A band that formed on my college campus while I was studying there

2. Farley, *Wounding and Healing*, 37.

took the name Sinner Fiend, an epithet meant to evoke a God whose passion for us constituted addiction. This is not what the ancients meant.

The idea that there are passions permeates fourth-century ascetic theology. A general description of them can be found in the *Praktikos*, by Evagrius Ponticus, a detailed ascetic theology. In keeping with other ascetic writers, Evagrius understands the monastic life as one of constant warfare with demonic influences that stir up passions. These passions are movements of the soul, rooted in the body. Evagrius describes eight distinct categories: gluttony, impurity, avarice, sadness, anger, *acedia*, vainglory, and pride.[3] The list corresponds roughly—with the elision of vainglory and pride—to the seven deadly sins but the passions are also not sins. They may be occasions for sin but they are not sin itself. Wendy Farley beautifully articulates this distinction between passion and sin:

> Passions distort everything they touch, including our emotions and our genuine impulses toward good. It is not our virtues but the divine image in us that matters. The passions are obstacles to the shining of this holy luminescence.[4]

Farley's words line up perfectly with Evagrius's eight passions. Gluttony induces the monk to give up his fasting under the guise of a wholesome concern about health. Impurity is an indiscriminate lust after bodies so strong the monk begins to think that practicing chastity is getting him nowhere. Avarice is less about greed than it is about concern for the future and the shame of dependency. It "suggests to the mind a lengthy old age, inability to perform manual labor (at some future date), famines that are sure to come, sickness that will visit us, the pinch of poverty, the great shame that comes from accepting the necessity of life from others."[5]

Sadness turns thoughts to home and family, to a former life and the pleasure and pain of nostalgia—both the longing for home and the regret at having chosen to leave. Anger accompanies sadness. It is a constant irritation that interferes particularly with prayer, as it nurses the indignation of a real or merely perceived insult or injury. *Acedia* is a restless boredom that seems to have as much in common with monastic life as it does with modern life. Evagrius tells us this is the most serious trouble of all for a monk. *Acedia* lengthens the day interminably; time drags. The

3. Evagrius, *Praktikos*, 16.
4. Farley, *Wounding and Healing*, 39.
5. Evagrius, *Praktikos*, 17.

monk begins to hate the place, to hate the life. It colors perception of the community, which seems suddenly lacking. This is the demon that drives the monk from place to place, as if the problem were external rather than internal—yet another distortion. Vainglory is more subtle. It seeks praise. It makes struggles public and predicts great success. When these vain hopes are dashed, pride enters. The monk suffering from pride misperceives himself by forgetting that God is the source of his virtue. The monk likewise misperceives his brothers, faulting them for their fail- ure to acknowledge his accomplishments. Pride was regarded by Aquinas as a cardinal vice, opening the way to other sins. Pride is not a vice but a passion here, but it is a gateway to further damage:

> Anger and sadness follow on the heels of this demon, and last of all there comes in its train the greatest of maladies—derangement of mind, associated with wild ravings and hallucinations of whole multitudes of demons in the sky.[6]

In this terrifying and colorful passage, Evagrius provides a template for what comes of the passions, left unchecked. It is nothing less than total madness.

The passions are not sin for Evagrius but rather temptation. At root, they induce the monk to give up his life by suggesting that it is either not worthwhile or by suggesting that another manner of life would be more prudent or fruitful. A story about Anthony illustrates the relationship between passion and sin:

> When Abba Anthony lived in the desert he was beset by *accidie*, and attacked by many sinful thoughts. He said to God, "Lord, I want to be saved but these thoughts do not leave me alone; what shall I do in my affliction? How can I be saved?" A short while afterwards, when he got up to go out, Anthony saw a man like himself sitting at his work, getting up from his work to pray, then sitting down and plaiting a rope, then getting up again to pray. It was an angel of the Lord sent to correct and reassure him. He heard the angel saying to him, "Do this and you will be saved." At these words, Anthony was filled with joy and courage. He did this, and he was saved.[7]

The passion—in this story, *acedia*—permits the infiltration of a series of sinful thoughts. Anthony is no longer sure of his life. It is boring, a drudge,

6. Evagrius, *Praktikos*, 20.

7. *Sayings*, 1–2.

and now he is not sure that any good is coming of his work. The story implicitly instructs anyone struggling with this question to pray to God—a standard remedy in the face of the passions. Anthony prays and asks God to answer the questions posed by the passions. Rather than listening to them and simply being carried away, he asks God to clarify. The answer he receives verifies that his way of life is the way of life he should pursue. Anthony experienced a passion here and was attacked by sinful thoughts but he did not sin because he took refuge in prayer.

Anthony's request for clarification is a crucial piece of the story because it illustrates the role of reason. The passions themselves are not sinful but allowing the passions to directly influence behavior is the wrong path. It is the path Evagrius tells us leads to madness—that is, to the total depravation of reason. Anthony reasons his way out of the passions, so to speak, by testing whether what he was feeling was in line with God's will, accessed through prayer.

Roberta Bondi's discussion is illuminating on this point. The passions as discussed here are rooted in a different psychology than the one we embrace and have little, if anything, to do with what we would normally call passion, which may be something like a particularly strong emotion. In this ancient psychology,

> The passions are the opposite of reason. Love . . . is linked with reason, not opposed to it. Reason *serves* love. Love draws reason to the good, to God. We moderns assume that love blinds because we believe that somehow we see people as they really are only when we see them at their worst.
>
> For the ancients, the reverse was true. When we see people as God sees them—that is, through the lens of infinite compassion—that is when we see the truth. Thus, they concluded that "this kind of vision . . . is essential to being truly rational."[8]

The person who exists in a state of *apatheia* is a person whose passions and appetites are governed by reason, where reason mediates love.

A WAY OF LIFE AND A WAY OF DEATH

Apatheia is the goal of the Christian life in desert monasticism because perfect *apatheia* is freedom from sin. Even as I write this, I recognize that, in Darcey Steinke's words, "it's old-fashioned to talk about sin, nutty

8. Bondi, *To Love*, 61.

and extreme, like a tent preacher damning the local prostitutes."[9] And it would be nutty to talk about sin with anything like the definition of sin you'd find in the vocabulary of a tent preacher. The thing is, as Steinke points out, the popular notion of sin is itself extreme and therefore not very useful. It's comfortable and easy to condemn a prostitute, a rapist, or murderer if I'm assured I'm not guilty of any of those things. Sin is part of those stories but sin is also something much less drastic—and consequently much more dangerous. In Steinke's words, "sin . . . consists of mundane daily acts that separate me from my own goodness and therefore from God."[10]

I would add to Steinke that when I am separated from my own goodness and from God, I am less than fully human. When we use the phrase "only human," we're telling ourselves a story about what it means to be a human being. Most of the time, "only human" covers our sins. Sinning is only human because it's only human to do the wrong thing. We aren't perfect, we tell ourselves. We can't be. We're only human. When we do wrong, we cover it with our humanity as if doing wrong and being a human being went hand in hand. There is a genuine insight in this. Failure is common to human beings. Every single person fails. Anecdotal evidence bears this out. Paul makes it explicit in his letter to the Romans: all have sinned. The experience of meaning well and trying to do right only to fail is one that every person can recognize.

But it is not human to sin. It cannot be human to sin if it is human to be divine. If we take seriously the Christian insistence that human beings were created uniquely in the image of God, then there is some sense in which it is true. It is not human to sin because it is human to be divine.

On the surface, this is a wild affirmation of humanity. It might even be scandalous. Do I deny that humanity is fallen? Do I reject that human beings are depraved? Do I mean to overlook sin by affirming an original goodness? The answer to all of these question is a resounding no. Although there is an affirmation of human goodness here, there is also a challenge. I affirm first the goodness of humanity and recall that, because we were created good, we retain something of that original blessing. But there is a vast distance between this vision of humankind as it is meant to be and the reality of what we are. The reason we tell ourselves sin is only

9. Steinke, *Easter Everywhere*, 177.

10. Ibid.

human is that we are so caught in it that we can't make our way from the pain and futility we all experience to the freedom and peace of pure love.

Theological positions that idealize humanity often downplay grace. If we are not fallen, if we still dwell in original perfection, there is no need for grace. There is also no real explanation for sin. We could overlook pain, pretend that suffering is always good, or even ignore evil altogether. In terms of Christian spirituality, the idea of original perfection without a concurrent narrative of original sin easily lends itself to rigorism. Put more simply, if we were born perfect and we are not fallen but we still sin, we are fully responsible for that sin. We ought to resist sin of our own efforts—and if we are not fallen, then it is in our power to resist sin. Far from denigrating humanity, the doctrine of original sin can act as a release valve for the pressure of our own expectations for ourselves. Because we are caught in original sin, our own efforts to resist sin will always fail. This is only a cause for despair if not for the possibility of grace.

But if we take seriously that what humankind needs most is restoration, grace must also be reconfigured. Grace is not primarily a reprieve from eternal judgment and punishment. It is a healing agent that restores humanity to its original wholeness. The goal of the incarnation was not to save us from God's wrath but rather to renew the human race. In order to restore us to our original perfection as creatures in the image of God, God's perfect image took flesh. This opened the possibility of a release from sin into a healing that begins here and now. This is not the fruit of human effort. It is not the realization of something that was already there. It is a new hope that we can be made whole and healthy again in cooperation with the working of the Holy Spirit in our lives.

Sin is arranging my bus route to avoid the homeless. I do this as if they were obstacles to my comfort instead of human beings. At best, I see them as entertaining stories. At worst, stray animals. In all ways I fail to respond to them as full human beings. And when I do that, I make myself something less than human.

Cooperating with the Holy Spirit in my own restoration begins with recognizing that my actions are sinful. It continues with the passions because they name the internal process that prompts me to sin without even thinking. And if I can name what ails me, it can be cured.

FACING MY DEMONS

The passions described by Evagrius are at times almost uncannily modern. The noon-day demon that afflicts monks with restless boredom and prompts them to check again, just one more time, to see if anyone is coming down the road is surely the driving force behind Twitter and Facebook. Even so, much of what Evagrius describes is endemic to a particular time, place, and way of life—none of which is anything like my life. I experience restless boredom but my real struggle is finding time and space for silence. The Egyptian monk surely had an abundance of silence and solitude and therefore the greater struggle with restlessness. Ordinary men and women certainly experience an indiscriminate desire for bodies but those who have committed wholly to celibacy have the greater struggle. This is true of all the passions. There is a necessary act of translation that accounts above all for scale. This is because of the fundamental difference between a secular life and a monastic one.

Not only that but the assumptions of the ancient world don't always match those of the modern world. This was already evident in ancient ideas about the passions, which are rooted in a distinctive ancient psychology.[11] The demonic is a commonly cited point of difference between ancient and modern. The Abbas and Ammas have quite a bit to say about demons, as does Athanasius. In his *Life of Anthony*, Athanasius accounts for the ability of some to predict the future by attributing it to demons, who have light, subtle bodies and are able to run more quickly than human beings and can therefore tell in advance who is coming down the road.[12] For modern people, the idea that there are self-directed beings composed of a subtle material wandering the earth unseen is pretty hard to accept.

The concept of the demonic is too central to desert monasticism to simply jettison and, as a theological category, the demonic accounts for things we could not otherwise name effectively. Alexander Schmemann makes this case in the classic text, *For the Life of the World*. He writes:

> According to some modern interpreters of Christianity, "demonology" belongs to an antiquated world view and cannot be taken seriously by the man who "uses electricity." We cannot argue with them here. What we must affirm, what the Church has always affirmed, is that the use of electricity may be "demonic," as in fact

11. Bondi, *To Love*, 59–62.
12. Athanasius, *Life of Anthony*, 55.

may be the use of anything and of life itself. That is, in other words, the experience of evil which we call *demonic* is not that of a mere absence of good, or, for that matter, of all sorts of existential alienations and anxieties. It is indeed the *presence* of dark and irrational power. Hatred is not merely absence of love. It is certainly more than that, and we recognize its presence as an almost physical burden that we feel in ourselves when we hate. In our world in which normal and civilized men "used electricity" to exterminate six million human beings . . . the "demonic" reality is not a myth.[13]

In other words, what the concept of the demonic describes is a human intuition that there is a substantial, active aspect of evil. Evil is nothing, but, to borrow language from Karl Barth, it is not *merely* nothing but rather *Das Nachtige*—that is, nothingness. This is evil as a substantial nothing, annihilating worlds as it rolls across the sky, as in the children's film *The Neverending Story*. In such cases, it is not enough to refer to personal evil or sin. The depth of the destruction and the force of its desire to undo and wreak destruction truly deserves the name demonic.

Schmemann alludes here to the association that is frequently made between the demonic and the inner life of a human being, which can be characterized by a struggle with what we might call personal demons. He insists that the demonic is more than this but in the passions, the demonic interfaces directly with interior life in a way that does resonate with the idea of a psychological demon. Whether or not we accept the existence of demons as a physical reality, the demonic is a useful template for understanding what it's like to be a human being, as described in early ascetic theology. This is primarily how Wendy Farley understands the demonic. She is just the sort of modern interpreter Schmemann has in mind, arguing that it is "anachronistic, to say the least, to appeal to the 'demons' as the source of our difficulties," but Farley also recognizes that if taken metaphorically, the demons represent the "ways our minds become our enemies, inflicting us with a kind of internal oppression that mirrors harm done to us in the external world."[14] She therefore concludes that the demons are not physical realities but rather refer to the

inner workings of mind that can sometime feel as if they were alien forces. They symbolize the paradox of wishing for good but becoming entangled in evil. The demons are famous for their talents at

13. Schmemann, *Life of the World*, 69–70.
14. Farley, *Wounding and Healing*, 73.

> seduction and deception. They seduce us with a promise for some
> sweet good: wealth, nourishment, beauty, wisdom, love. But the
> demons' promises conceal some nasty, often fatal, surprise.[15]

Farley appeals to the penetrating psychological insight of the Abbas and
Ammas. The way they describe demonic forces resonates with the ordinary experience of struggling to do good against what can sometimes
feels like a dark passenger. It is not enough to merely want to do good
or to try to do it. Some deeper wisdom is needed to distinguish between
what is really good and what is evil in disguise.

If asked whether demons as such are real—that is, the physical existence of demons as beings with personalities—Farley and Schmemann
would likely give opposing answers. Farley clearly does not believe in the
physical existence of demons and Schmemann arguably does. Even so,
both participate in the same act of translation between ancient and modern. The wisdom encoded in ancient ways of viewing the world is just as
applicable for us as it was in its own time.

I experience the physical sensations of passion that lead predictably
to self- or other-destructive actions, just as Evagrius describes. He also
acknowledges that each of us struggles with one or more of the passions
above the others, which I also know to be true of myself. When I was
younger, my struggle was with gluttony. I had an eating disorder as a
young woman, which I call gluttony because the passion is about an un-
due fixation with food rather than overindulgence in it. I rarely indulged
my desire to eat and yet most of my thoughts were about food. Would I
eat? If not, how would I hide that from the people around me? If I did,
what would I eat and how much? I kept a tally on calories consumed and
I engaged in careful and secretive practices to hide my food intake. At
night, I measured the circumference of arms, thighs, calves, waist—just to
be sure everything was in order. I didn't eat enough to nourish my body
appropriately and yet food was my life.

As the gluttony receded, I discovered I was very angry. In some
ways, anger is a straightforward passion. Identifying its destructive nature
is relatively easy. I was so given to anger—and still am in some ways—that
a relatively innocuous stimulus could provoke an outsized response. A
comment or a look or a minor disappointment could elicit a harsh word
or even a tirade. Like Jesus, the Abbas and Ammas pair anger and murder.

15. Ibid.

In modern psychological terms, my anger was misplaced. I was justifiably angry about certain events in my history. Because I had never processed those feelings, they stayed with me, overflowing into misdirected rage. In Evagrian terms, the passion of anger overwhelmed me. I never considered the source or the target of my anger. I simply experienced this movement of the soul and I acted without any intervening mediation of my rational faculty. Rationally, I might have known my anger wasn't really about the person who had offended me and I might have held back from saying and doing some of the things I've done out of anger.

Eventually, I became less angry and I realized I was deeply sad. In his discussion of sadness, Evagrius is careful to distinguish between a healthy grief—he has in mind primarily grief over our own sins—from sadness. The essence of sadness is a kind of fascination with the past. It is a relentless grief over things that cannot be helped or changed. For the Abbas and Ammas, it was grief over a life that might have been if they hadn't fled to the desert. They think of children that might have come and experiences they could have shared.

In some ways, this is very peculiar to monastic experience but it is also applicable to modern life as "a kind of grief for what has been given up for the sake of the present life."[16] There are always choices regretted, roads not taken, sacrifices made. It is easy to feel like we took a wrong turn somewhere and the habit of dwelling on what could have been if we'd made a different choice is recognizably destructive.

Our cultural fascination with the idea of time-travel speaks to this. A different choice yields a wholly altered reality. A single moment changed could produce an entirely new world. Present unhappiness can be undone by redoing the past. As an imaginative trope, time-travel is about reliving the past in a way that allows us to change it.

The vacuity of the impulse is brilliantly parodied in the film *Napoleon Dynamite*. Uncle Rico is just sure that if he could go back to 1982 and win his high school football championship, he'd be a professional football player with a mansion instead of an itinerant Tupperware salesman living in an orange van. In his actual life, his obsession with the past interferes with his relationships. His longtime girlfriend has left him because he's still trying to relive his glory days. All he can think is that in his imaginary life, he'd be happily married to his soulmate. The character is funny

16. Bondi, *To Love*, 73.

because the audience understands how ridiculous Rico's fixation on 1982 really is. The story arc culminates with his attempt at time-travel using a device that sits between the legs and delivers a jolt of electricity directly to the groin.[17]

Uncle Rico is a caricature of a recognizable phenomenon, one that resonates with Evagrius's understanding of sadness. The amalgam of self-pity and blame that keeps him inured to the past is comical but I see myself in it. For me, the chief regret is professional. I hear a word or a comment, or I have a thought that prompts me to look at my career and recognize its failures. I grieve for the things that could have been if only this or that had been different, if only I'd made some other choice. I experience a welling up of pain in the center of my chest. It's a warm, queasy feeling. It extends from the sternum down to the pit of my stomach. This is the movement of my soul. Without thinking, I dive into a river of thoughts, one following on the other. The year on the job market that came to nothing. The years spent working as an adjunct for very little pay. The foolish choice I made in my profession and how I might have been happier doing something else. The program I chose and the idiosyncratic path I took through it. The advice I ignored that might have made me a more marketable candidate now. The dissertation I should have written. My working-class childhood and its lack of educational resources. The hometown I left behind to become an academic. The foolish idea that I could compete with men and women who had the best of everything growing up and move through academia like it's their native country. I'm never going to be more than a backward foreigner, which is all the evidence I need to regret my choice to pursue an academic career in the first place, to say nothing of a thousand wrongs turns along the way.

It all begins with that pinprick of thought. This stimulus produces a movement of the soul. I experience it physically. More often than not, I am overwhelmed by it and it takes over my thoughts. I argue with it rationally but the passion is stronger than my reason. In fact, the Abbas and Ammas tell me that arguing with it is a way of indulging it, which gives it strength. The more I argue with it, the more it draws me into a feedback loop of worry and regret, of guilt and even shame. I am every bit as self-indulgent and ridiculous as Uncle Rico. My conviction that I should have chosen a different graduate program sounds less laughable

17. Hess, "Business Partners," Napoleon Dynamite.

than his conviction that things would be different if he'd won a football game in 1982, but underneath it's exactly the same.

BEYOND TRADITION

The great gift of Farley's work on the passions in *The Wounding and Healing of Desire: Weaving Heaven and Earth* is her creativity. She doesn't limit herself to what Evagrius said. Instead, she opens her framework to human experience itself. Desire is the crux of the project. Human souls long so soundly that they are wounded by the sheer force of the longing. They are "but incarnate flames of desire," to quote Farley's wonderfully evocative opening phrase.[18] The desire we know as human burns us because it must consume. And consume it does. Desire consumes everything in the world because, at bottom, its goal is infinite. It can never be sated by the merely finite. It can only be satisfied in God. The problem of desire, insofar as there is one, is misdirection. Desire causes suffering because we forget that God is the only thing that can sate us. Misused and misdirected, desire consumes to our harm. The unspoken word beneath Abba Poemanʼs aphorism is simply this: Only God can satisfy. Everything else fails.

From this beginning point, she creates a distinctive view of the passions as "habituated obstacles that take root in the human soul, blocking us from our heart's desire," which is God.[19] Although the passions are not, strictly speaking, habits in the understanding of the desert fathers and mothers, Farley is in absolute agreement with them when she argues that the passions are not fleeting experiences. They are something much deeper than that, which means they are much more difficult to overcome than it might seem. It is not a simple thing to just stop doing wrong and no amount of telling ourselves to snap out of it can change what is deeply rooted in our individual and collective ways of being.

Farley recognizes that ways of being—even mistaken ways—have a local aspect. They belong to a particular time and place. And for that reason, although it's possible to translate Evagrian passions into modern terms, she names passions that belong to the modern world. She first names terror. It may hide itself, as passions often do, but there are always hints: "an inordinate fear of harm to oneself or others or a fear that pops

18. Farley, *Wounding and Healing*, 1.
19. Farley, *Wounding and Healing*, 55.

up in odd places."[20] If I can use myself as an example, this sort of terror might manifest itself in flinging oneself through the open door of the bus in order to escape a happy homeless guy who's asking you for your phone number, apparently because he thinks this is funny. I confess that some part of my decision to change bus routes arose from just this passion of terror. It is an out of balance fear that people who have shown themselves harmless to this point will suddenly turn sinister in the middle of a well-populated public place. It is not rational. To the contrary, it overwhelms my reason, which tells me I have no reason for fear. And I call it a passion because it overturns my rational mind and dictates actions that are contrary to love.

Farley's willingness to extend the tradition is welcome. Nothing in Evagrius directly addresses the time I jumped off the bus and yet I recognize it as sin. Moreover, I recognize her description of terror as a genuine description of something awry in modern life. She goes on to name rage and addiction as passions that characterize modern life and I follow her lead in naming a passion of my own: revulsion.

Revulsion often begins with an external stimulus. There is an un-washed stink, the smell of urine, feces, sweat, or alcohol. There are sights that gall me: toenails unclipped, nose hairs untamed, or diseases of skin. There are off-color jokes, coughing fits, and people who sit too close to me. Whatever the stimulus, it is like a pinprick that produces a movement of the soul I experience viscerally as nausea. It's a warm feeling that knots my stomach and wells from there to the base of my throat. My mouth waters and I turn away. In my worst moments, I do not hide this reaction from the human being whose presence has prompted it and he or she sees clearly how disgusted I am. I am revolted and I allow that sensation to dictate my behavior.

It is better, I tell myself, if I avoid the situation altogether. But this is giving in to my sin. It is abdicating my humanity in favor of reacting without thinking. This is a mundane story but it's also what bondage to sin looks and sounds like. I am caught in a way of reacting that separates me from my own better impulses. So long as my revulsion dictates how I behave, I am little better than a dog, reacting without thinking.

20. Farley, *Wounding and Healing*, 59.

chapter seven
Tyrone

Abba, give me a word.

Abba Poeman said, "Teach your mouth to say
that which is in your heart."[1]

As I approached the bus stop, I saw two men sitting on the bench.
One of them wore a filthy trucker's cap. His hair was roughly the
color of steel, gray and greasy. The lines around his eyes told a
story about too many days in the sun and his shoulders hunched forward.
He almost looked like he was asleep. The other man seemed younger than
his friend. His complexion was very dark, almost blue. He was wearing
a flannel shirt and sweatpants in spite of the heat. He leaned back in his
seat, roughly the shape of a bullfrog, and held a plastic sack in his hand.

I came up from behind them and stood by the end of the bench,
watching the road to the north for the bus. The bullfrog man startled.
"Where'd you come from?" he all but shouted. The man in the trucker's
cap laughed. "She was back there," he said.

"You were? You're so quiet!" The bullfrog man paused for effect and
then said again, "You were so quiet! Where did you come from? You're
like a ghost."

I am like a ghost, I thought. *White.* I laughed. "I cut across the grass
right there," I said as I pointed to the place. "I guess you missed me."

"You know what she's like? You're like that movie where the people
just pop up out of nowhere. You know what I'm talking about?" I didn't
and neither did the man in the trucker's cap, but we all laughed and I
turned my face north again to see if the bus was coming.

I didn't want to talk anymore. Conversations on the bus get tricky
for me very quickly. Bus small talk usually involves asking people where
they're headed. Most people assume I'm a student at St. Edward's, where

---

1. *Sayings*, 175.

I work as an adjunct. I have to explain that I'm actually an instructor and yes, I am old enough for that. Then they want to know what I teach and whether I say religion or theology, the conversation turns a corner. What comes next is anyone's guess. It could be anything from a screed about the hypocrisy of organized religion to a detailed account of a peyote experience. I wasn't in the mood, so I pulled my headphones out of my bag and started to put them on.

Before I had a chance, the bullfrog man asked me if I was on my way to school. I thought about lying but I liked him, so I decided against it. I told him I was on my way to teach a class and when he asked me what I teach, I told him the truth. The course was a basic introduction to Christianity, which I taught by reviewing the history and development of major doctrines.

His reaction was hard to read. He grunted and slumped back on his bench but he seemed to be thinking about something. Then he asked me if I'm a Christian. I told him I was. The man in the trucker's hat chimed in with an Amen. He was a Christian, too, apparently.

The bullfrog man was quiet again and then he said, "Whatchyoutinkboutmuslims?" He said it like it was all one word and I couldn't make sense of it, so I squinted and leaned forward.

"I'm sorry?"

"WhatchyouthinkboutMUSLIMS?"

"Oh, Muslims! You're asking about Islam."

"Yeah, Islam. You know about Islam?"

"A little," I said. It's hardly my area of expertise but I know more than most people.

"So what about these Muslims they got over in the place with Muammar Gaddafi? Where is that, Libya? What about them Muslims?"

I stopped to consider this because Islam is a tinderbox and Libya was not something I felt prepared to discuss at the bus stop. I decided on something relatively neutral. "Islam is a beautiful religion," I started. "It's complex, though. There are some wonderful things about it and it can be very peaceful." I hesitated. "But there's also the potential for violence."

"Amen," his friend said. "There's definitely violence. That's for sure." This was true, of course, but Islam is hardly unique in this respect. The bullfrog man was even harder to read this time. He grunted again and slumped. I decided to say more. "My point isn't that Islam is violent. It's just that it's too simple to say it's all about peace. Islam is about peace.

At the same time, some people use Islam to justify violence and that isn't good."

He grunted again, a bullfrog wrapped in an enigma.

"And you're a Christian?" he finally said. I told him I was.

"Amen, amen," said the man in the trucker's hat.

"Why'd you decide to study?"

"I guess I just had a lot of questions after college, so I went to seminary."

"Hmmm! Amen, amen!" I had a fan in the peanut gallery.

"You went to seminary?" He leaned back and looked me up and down. He looked amused but seemed impressed. Lots of people react with incredulity when I say I've been to seminary. I don't know if it's my age, my gender, or both, but it's a consistent reaction.

"Yeah, I went to seminary and then I did my PhD. Now I teach."

"Good for you," said the man in the trucker's hat.

"So you believe God is a man." It wasn't a question.

"No. That's not what I think."

"Yeah, you think God a is man, don't you?" Now it was a question. I was emphatic about my answer. "God is not a man," I said. And then I added, "except in Christ."

"Amen, amen. Jesus was a man," said the man in the trucker's hat.

"Right," I went on, "so God was incarnate as a man in Jesus—and Jesus was clearly male—but God? God is not a man. God is not a woman. God is beyond gender."

The bullfrog man nodded appreciatively and said nothing more. The bus pulled up to the curb and the three of us fumbled for our passes and filed onto it. I sat down next to a college student and the bullfrog man sat in front of me. For the first time, I caught his odor. The flannel and the sweats amplified the sweat and he smelled vaguely of urine. He fell to talking with his seatmate, also a college student. When we reached UT, his seatmate got off and the bullfrog man turned back to me. He looked me in the eye, pointed at the seat across the aisle, and said, "Sit down."

I don't necessarily do that well with strangers who issue commands like that but for some reason, I obeyed him. The bus lurched back into motion.

"I'm Tyrone."

Tyrone, I thought. *A person with a name.*

He wanted my name and I told him. Then he said, "Annie, I'm about to teach you something about Islam." My stomach contracted in a knot. I shifted uncomfortably in my seat but I sat quietly and listened.

"You know about Islam?" he asked.

"A little," I said.

"You learn it off of TV?"

That made me laugh. I couldn't think of a worse way to learn about a religion, especially Islam. I told him I learned it from books and from a class I took once at a mosque and I told him which mosque. He broke out in a grin. "Heyyyy! I go there! That's my mosque!" He smiled, white teeth against dark skin, and I smiled, too.

"I just love our imam," he went on. The imam is a slender Egyptian-American man who might be thirty but is probably not much older than that. He asked me if I'd met him and I said I had. "He is a very good man. Very spiritual and very keen powers of mind." He pointed to his forehead with both hands.

"Yes," I said. "I was very impressed with him."

"My Muslim name is Yaseen."

Yaseen.

"You know Nation of Islam is not Islam, right?" It came straight out of left field. "Okay," I said.

"It's not the real Islam. My father was from Kenya." He seemed to have a hard time staying with the thread but I wasn't prepared to argue with him about it. "My father," he went on, "see, my mother was a Christian woman. Do you know Farrakhan?" I nodded. "Okay, I met him this one time. He came to my father's house and I told him, let me sit you down and teach you about real Islam."

He leaned in close to my face and looked me square in the eyes. His face was wide around his tiny bloodshot eyes. I could smell the sweat on him but I didn't move. "I don't believe there's no God who's a black man and there's any white devils. I don't think so. That's what I said. And you know what else I said?" He was still close. I shook my head. "God," he said. "You know, God. God's love is like sunlight and it falls on everybody. And peace. Peace is for everybody and God's love. That's Islam."

He sat back in his seat with a grunt and was quiet. I suddenly realized I was tense, clutching the handles of my bag in my lap. I relaxed and stole a look at him. He caught my eye. "Do you understand?" he said.

"Sure," I replied, and Tyrone burst out laughing out of nowhere. I startled this time but I don't think he noticed. He wasn't looking at me anymore, caught up as he was in his reminiscence. "You know what he said to me? He said, 'You taught me something here today.'" He put on a ridiculous voice as he said it. "Figure that! I taught something to Mr. Farrakhan." He said the name with mock grandeur as if to say *Mr. Farrakhan who thinks he's something special.* I said nothing and he leaned back further.

"You know what else I told him?" I waited but he said nothing. Then he said, "I had me a wife one time."

"Did you?" I leaned forward, genuinely interested. He turned back toward me. "I did. We were married for twenty years. Twenty years," he sighed. "She died."

"I'm so sorry."

"That's when I got real sick. You know. And this." He made a vague motion with his hand.

"Oh."

"I had another wife, too."

"Oh?"

"My father was from Kenya, you know, so he found me this wife. She wanted to be my wife, so, you know. But I wasn't sure about her."

"No?"

"You know," he started to laugh again. "She had this . . . this . . . she used to put on all this." He made a circular motion over his face. "All this here. What you call it? All this," he paused for effect, "paint." He laughed hard and then he squinted at me, trying to gauge how much makeup I had on my face. "Hoo! She went around with all this on her face and then," he made a motion over his head indicating a hijab. He threw back his head and cackled. "And I said to her, you wearing all this," hand over face, "and then this," hand over head, "and woman, you scare me!"

I laughed, more to be polite and because he was so tickled than because I thought it was funny. He leaned back in and I smelled him again. "I told her, you look like a suicide bomber." He laughed some more. I definitely didn't think it was funny anymore. As he said this he reached back and pulled the wire for his stop.

"What's your name again?" he asked me as he gathered himself.

"Annie. And you're Tyrone, Yaseen." He looked surprised when I said it, but he nodded.

"Annie, you keep spreading the peace and the love," he said.

"I will," I assured him.

"You're doing good, then." He shook my hand and he was gone.

The absence of judgment is the presence of love.

chapter eight
The Living Dead

Abba, give me a word.

Abba James said, "It is better to receive hospitality
than to offer it."[1]

O N DECEMBER 18, 2008, I was in the car with my family driving
through Fredericksburg, Texas, on the way to visit family for the
Christmas holidays when we heard a report on KUT, the local
NPR affiliate, about Jennifer Gale. "It's her!" I told my husband. "This is
the woman I told you about. She's the one I met on the bus." I turned up
the volume and listened to Jennifer sing "Silent Night" in her uncertain
but earnest warble.

Jennifer is well known in Austin, mostly for her various political
campaigns. She ran for mayor a handful of times, city council, and even
the school board of the Austin Independent School District. In every
election, she won some percentage of the vote. Austin doesn't just shop
weird. We vote weird, too.

I met her on the bus on my way home from teaching. It was my first
semester working as an adjunct instructor at St. Edward's and it didn't
seem to be going very well. The course was unfamiliar and my students
seemed surly. I was still tense about finishing my dissertation. The bus
ride was long. I felt anxious, bored, and lonely most days. I sat stiffly near
the front when Jennifer boarded, breathless and overheated.

"I just came from a city council meeting," she announced as she col-
lapsed in a heap beside me. "I'm running for mayor." Her tone was just
a little bit sly, almost like it was all a big joke. She wore white polyester
shorts, the kind my grandmother would have called culottes, and there
was a dirty white visor on her head. She tucked her bus pass into her
fanny pack and leaned back. She was just scruffy enough to make me

1. *Sayings*, 104.

think she was probably homeless but I wasn't sure. She sighed and smiled at me and then she took a piece of chocolate out of the plastic sack she carried. She looked at the chocolate and then at me.

"Do you want some?" she offered hesitantly.

"No, thanks."

"Oh, good!" she burst out. "No offense," she said with a grin, "but I was really looking forward to this. Now I don't have to share." She laughed as she placed the chocolate delicately on her tongue. It was a big, infectious laugh and I found myself laughing, too.

We rode and she told me about her bid for mayor. Her platform was about health and wellness. She told me she had a dream—the whole city training for an iron man triathlon. "You know what I mean?" she asked and I nodded even though I wasn't sure I did. "It's where you do the 26.2 miles running, 112 miles biking, and the uh . . ." she searched mentally for a number. "I forget but you swim." She trailed off.

"I've heard of that," I volunteered.

Her eyes brightened. "You have? Then you know what I mean! Can you imagine?" she gushed. "A whole city training together and running all together!"

I pictured a mass of people in running shorts making their way across the South Congress bridge. It made me smile.

"It's my health care plan," she said. "Don't you think we'd be healthier?" Before I could agree, she added, "I think it would be good for crime, too." She seemed thoughtful for a moment. Then she turned to me, childlike, and asked if I thought it was a good idea.

"Yeah," I said. "I mean, sure." It sounded weak but she took it.

"Then you'll vote for me. Remember my name: Jennifer Gale."

Jennifer Gale.

As we listened to KUT that morning, I assumed the report had something to do with her political ambitions. I chattered happily to my husband about our meeting on the bus and what a wonderful and weird person she was. I fell silent just in time to hear the conclusion of the report:

"Jennifer Gale was found dead on the morning of December 17th."

I burst into tears. She was my friend.

I later learned that Jennifer died on the steps of the First English Lutheran Church. It's the kind of detail you couldn't add to a fictional story about a homeless transgendered woman without straining your credibility.

As if that weren't enough, an eerily prophetic video surfaced of her last appearance before the Austin city council. In it, she sings "Silent Night"— the same rendition we heard on KUT that morning—and she introduces the same health care plan she pitched to me on the bus. She tells the council members that our newspaper obituaries are filled with young people, people gone too soon, whose deaths could have been prevented by proper health care. It was recorded the day before she died of heart failure at the age of 48.

In the midst of life, we are in death. There is nothing I know that is more true than this.

RESTING IN HOPE

Death is sure. In the face of all my doubts, it is a reliable certainty. I will someday die. This does not make me special. The story of every living thing encompasses death because it is our nature as finite things to whither and die. This is what we call to mind each Ash Wednesday: "Remember that you are but dust and to dust you shall return." This is an incontrovertible truth of our experience. This is the horror and the beauty of the cosmos. It is the pain of the merciful heart "burning for the sake of all creation, for [human beings], for birds, for animals . . . and for every created thing."[2] Everything living will someday die and there is no stopping it. There is only waiting and hoping.

But there is hope, and death is not the worst thing that can happen. One of the most compelling parts of the Christian story for me is its account of death. I don't mean a glib promise of an afterlife. There is something more—a promise that from the wreck of death, new life can spring up. There is the promise of a new life after death and immortality, with Christ's death as the first fruits. In Paul's words, "if Christ is not risen, your faith is futile," and if our faith is futile, then "those who have fallen asleep in Christ have perished" (1 Corinthians 15:17–18). Death is not the final word on human life. The God of the incarnation is a God who overturns all things, including the order of life and death. And when that order has been overturned, this God draws life from things that are dead. Without Christ, everything living slowly dies. In Christ, though we were dead, yet we shall live. By nature, everything dies, but in Christ, all things are new again—young, full of vigor and health. Without Christ, the living

2. Alfeyev, *Isaac the Syrian*, 43.

slowly die. In Christ, though you were dead, yet shall you live. This is the gospel in its simplest form.

This understanding of the incarnation has profound significance for a vision of sin. This is clear in Athanasius's account of the incarnation, which addresses death extensively. As Athanasius sees it, there would be no corruption without sin and without corruption, no death. Since the incarnation addresses the effects of sin—the ensuing corruption that threatens to destroy humanity—it is substantially about death.

The story begins with creation. The world and everything in it was created by God through the Word. The incarnation is nothing less than the renewal of the whole creation—significantly this means not only humanity but the entire created order. This renewal must come through the same agent. In Athanasius's words: "the renewal of creation has been wrought by the Self-same Word Who made it in the beginning."[3] The serpent's deception was simple. God warned Adam and Eve that if they ate of the forbidden tree, they would die. The serpent convinced Eve it would not be. It was and the condition of our world is evidence of this fact: Adam and Eve not only died but were doomed with all their descendants to "remain in the state of death and corruption."[4]

The incarnation itself was intended to address this condition. This is an important difference from later views of the atonement that emphasize human transgression and the need for God's justice to be served or the need for someone to bear God's wrath, as if Jesus were some kind of cosmic wrath-absorbing sponge. Instead, Athanasius emphasizes the effects of sin, which had to be addressed in their own right. To put the point more directly, subverting God's need to punish someone doesn't solve the real problem.

To be clear, Athanasius would not have rejected the core idea of substitution, which does have its roots in the New Testament. The basic idea of substitution is simply that Christ was offered as a sacrifice on our behalf. This finds expression in Hebrews, among other books: "Christ, [has] been offered once to bear the sins of many" (Heb 9:28).

This view of the atonement leans on an understanding of sin as an individual and personal reality. Theologians who insist on it may have a doctrine of original sin but they don't see the incarnation itself as a

---

3. Athanasius, *On the Incarnation*, 26.

4. Ibid., 29.

way to address original sin. Instead, Christ's death makes it possible for human beings to get right with God, as it were. It reconciles humanity with God—itself a biblical image drawn from 2 Corinthians 5. This is what makes it possible for individuals to relate to God on a personal level. Without it, we are separated from God.

Athanasius would probably concur that sin separates us from God, in some sense, but the incarnation is more than a way for individuals to gain access to the divine. It is nothing less than the restoration of creation itself. Taken alone, a substitutionary view cannot answer every question: Why wasn't repentance enough? Without invoking the limiting effects of God's wrath or justice on God's forgiveness and love, Athanasius provides a simple answer for the question, why wasn't love enough? He writes:

> Had it been a case of trespass only, and not of subsequent corruption, repentance would have been well enough; but when once transgression had begun men came under the power of the corruption proper to their nature and were bereft of the grace which belonged to them as creatures in the Image of God.[5]

Disobedience is only the beginning. In fact, if our collective problem were really the need for forgiveness, there wouldn't be any need for an incarnation. God could simply forgive. But personal sin is a drop in the bucket of humanity's need for redemption. The very image of God— our very humanity—was being worn away by the effects of corruption. What we needed wasn't a way for God to forgive us. We needed complete healing—a restoration so total we can only call it resurrection from the dead. Only the incarnation of the Word is comprehensive enough to address the futility of mortality.

Athanasius draws this view of the atonement directly from Paul. In Romans, Paul outlines a theology of the atonement that works on precisely this cosmic scale. From being dead in sin, condemned by the law, we are renewed in baptism and become alive to Christ and dead to sin. But though we are alive in Christ, we still suffer the effects of sin. This means both that we suffer not only the effects of our own sins but the sins of others—indeed, the sins of the whole world. This is even better said the sin of the world, in the singular, since it is the cumulative effect of sin on the whole creation that the incarnation is meant to heal. The twisting distortion introduced into creation weighs on the whole creation.

5. Ibid., 33.

This is what Paul means when he writes, in Romans 8:18–21, of creation's redemption:

> I consider that the sufferings of this present time are not worth comparing with the glory that is to be revealed to us. For the creation waits with eager longing for the revealing of the sons of God; for the creation was subjected to futility, not of its own will but by the will of him who subjected it in hope; because the creation itself will be set free from its bondage to decay and obtain the glorious liberty of the children of God.

There is a peculiar resonance between Paul's words and the decidedly unromantic view Werner Herzog takes of nature in *The Burden of Dreams*, a documentary that follows the making of Herzog's film *Fitzcarraldo*. Faced with the near failure of his film, which was shot on location in the Amazon, Herzog describes creation as unfinished in the jungle. There is no collective harmony, he asserts, or rather if there is, it is what he calls "a harmony of overwhelming and collective murder."[6]

There is a violence about nature that we accept as ordinary and natural but which, speaking theologically, is not. Returning to Romans, Paul speaks of the creation groaning as if in labor, struggling to bring forth a new reality (see Rom 8:22). Herzog hears this groaning and feels the pangs of nature. Frederica Mathewes-Green describes the same insight in the work of another artist, a woman she calls Sheila. Mathewes-Green describes one of Sheila's paintings:

> Against a vague seascape of pale blue and rose is suspended a withered corpse, not human but animal. It is a cacophony, gray shreds of leather skin and narrow white bones. The harmony of the body is wildly disrupted, and a claw-tipped forearm appears to emerge from the ripped bag of abdomen. Behind the head a blue line levels the horizon, and above it floats a pale golden sky. The contrast of the distant tenderness of the background and the wracked torment of the corpse clears a space for quiet sorrow.[7]

The death and decay of an animal—in this case a squirrel—is emblematic of the corruption of nature itself. We accept the pain and sorrow that come with death as natural because, in Sheila's words, "we don't realize how much we've lost . . . how far we've fallen."[8]

6. *Burden of Dreams.*

7. Mathewes-Green, *Facing East,* 93.

8. Ibid., 94.

Human beings are a part of nature and suffer under the same burden of corruption as everything else. We are set apart because we were first in sin. It was through our sin that corruption and death entered the world. It was because of death that corruption and sin became part of our reality. These realities are intertwined. We suffer because we sin and we sin because we die. The wages of sin is death but the sting of death is sin. Without one, we would not suffer the other.

SIGNS OF LIFE

I suffer under the burden of my own sins and Jennifer Gale died under the weight of hers. I don't mean that her death was her own fault. Sin is too deep to make such a simple statement. But she nevertheless lived her life under the same burden of sin all human beings experience. This is the pain of the human condition: loneliness, sadness, sickness, death. She suffered the physical ailments that were native to her body, made worse by her circumstances. The ordinary aches and pains of aging were surely magnified by her exposure to the elements, sleeping in the wet and cold, walking everywhere she went, often in the hot sun. Even if she hadn't been homeless, Jennifer would have suffered. It can be difficult to find a place in the world as a transgendered person. The normal confusion that comes with a developing sexuality is easily amplified by social disapproval. And the vulnerability of transgendered persons is undeniable in a world that would rather see people in one clear-cut category or another.

She died alone, outside, without shelter or comfort. Like Leslie, she had some notoriety but no one inquired too closely into her conditions. It's not clear what it would mean to help her without violating her own desires. It's also possible that helping her would so alter her way of being in the world that it would destroy the wonderful way she related to perfect strangers. What is clear is that, although many people enjoyed her as a kind of carnival act, no one was with her when she died. It's unlikely anyone even realized she was sick.

For all that, meeting Jennifer changed something in me. In the midst of death, she was full of life. In the darkness of my own loneliness and discontent, she was a light. Her eyes shone. She was, in her way, beautiful. It wasn't her physical appearance that drew me in. It was something else, something lively that I can only call a sign of life.

When I heard of her death on the radio, I cried and then, as grieving people often do, I found myself spilling out a story about her, a story

about the day I met her on the bus. Shortly after she boarded, a couple in
their sixties got on the bus and sat across from her, shoulder to shoulder,
poring over a bus schedule.

"Where do you need to get?" Jennifer offered. The couple seemed
reticent to respond. *Tourists*, I thought. They didn't look sure they wanted
to chat with a friendly woman with a stubbly chin. But the man responded
anyway. They were on their way to UT to see their daughter.

"Oh, you're in luck. This is the bus." Jennifer's eyes lit up as she spoke.
"You just need to take this straight up to it. You can't miss it. But ask the
driver."

"Thank you." The man spoke without looking up. He folded the
schedule and crossed his arms and turned his face to the front of the
bus. Jennifer looked at him shyly and then she looked at me, sidelong.
"Anything else I can help you with?" she asked.

"No." He was firm.

"Hey, do you know when Friday comes before Thursday?"

The tourists looked like they weren't sure the question was for them.
The man looked up at her but said nothing. I wasn't sure it was for me,
either, so I said nothing. "In a dictionary!" Jennifer announced trium-
phantly. There was a split-second pause before everyone laughed. Even the
tourist with his arms crossed had to chuckle, shaking his head as he did.

Since then, I've encountered more than a few other self-appointed
bus entertainers. One of my favorite stories is about a particular homeless
man who struck up a conversation with a pretty red-headed woman. "You
Irish?" he asked. She nodded mutely. He yammered for a minute or two
about being Irish in a tone loud enough to get the attention of the whole
bus. Then he seemed to notice he had attention. "Hey," he asked her, still
loud enough to address everyone, "do you know how come the Arabs got
all the oil and the Irish got all the whisky?" There was a perfectly timed
beat of silence before he shouted, "We got first pick!" The bus exploded
into appreciative laughter. "Thank you, thank you," he added. "I'm here
all week!"

The out-of-towners were clearly unaccustomed to impromptu bus
joke-telling but they laughed and Jennifer clearly approved. "Okay, you're
getting it now," she said as she leaned forward a little and caught my eye
again. She had a look of mischief, the same look my four-year-old daughter gets when I'm mad and she's trying to make me laugh so I'll forget to

punish her. "So," she began again. "What did the pony say when it had a sore throat."

This time the man was game. "I don't know. What?"

"I'm a little horse." Jennifer giggled with sheer glee. I laughed, too. She shifted forward in her seat again and the man leaned back in his, loosening his arms and beginning to smirk. "Okay, one more for you. What do you call a shoe that's . . . wait, how is it? What do you call a shoe . . . yeah, that's it. What do you call a shoe that's made from a banana peel? A slipper!" The way she didn't wait for the punchline was utterly childish in the best possible sense. The man laughed in earnest.

"Your stop is coming up soon," Jennifer reassured him. "Where are you from?"

"Oregon."

"Ah, but what part of Oregon? Not Portland, surely."

"Oh, no. Not Portland. We're from Salem."

"I could tell you weren't from Portland. I don't mean any offense by that."

"None taken."

"It's just that Portland is kind of like Austin: weird."

"That's one word for it," the man replied wryly. It was Jennifer's turn to laugh.

"You just don't look like you're from that kind of place." She giggled and shot me a furtive glance to make sure I was in on the joke. The man agreed in a voice that was gruff but not unkind. They understood each other.

"Hey, I know where you should eat," Jennifer suddenly said. "Gatti's. They have them all over. I go in there all the time. It's really great food."

"Gotti's? What kind of food is it?"

"Gatti's. With an A. It's Italian but totally local. You'll love it. This is UT." We were pulling up to the curb, the sidewalk crammed with its usual throng of undergraduates. The tourists thanked Jennifer and stepped off the bus into the crowd. She sighed. "I like to be helpful when I can." She said it to no one in particular. Then she gathered her things and turned to me. "I'm glad I met you today," she said.

"Me, too," I replied. And it was true.

"Okay, so. Who are you going to vote for in the election?" By this time I'd forgotten all about Jennifer's bid for mayor. I stumbled over my answer and told her I wasn't sure yet. I didn't know anything about the candidates.

"Yes, you do!" she prompted. "Jennifer Gale." She enunciated each syllable carefully. "Remember that name."

"Okay, okay. I'll try."

"You have to say it. Just say, I'm voting for Jennifer Gale." She stood up.

"I'm voting for Jennifer Gale," I smiled up at her.

"Glad to know you!" She extended her hand and I shook it. And I smiled like an idiot the rest of the way home.

Jennifer got off the bus in the neighborhood of First English. I suppose she was going home but I didn't really think about it at the time. I wasn't even sure she was homeless. I wasn't sure of much about her—her gender, if she'd given me her real name, or if she was really running for mayor. I only knew I liked her. In those few moments on the bus, she'd managed to create something. She transformed all of us from random strangers into a community. People often say Leslie is Austin. I say Jennifer made Austin happen on that bus. A motley collection of people occupying the same space became something more, if only for a few minutes. And it was beautiful.

GROANING

I once overheard a pair of homeless men warn a pretty young woman not to ride the 1L/1M after dark. "We call this the big ballers express," one of them leered. "But seriously," he went on, "it's fine for us but it wouldn't be good for you. Just be careful out there 'cuz some of us is on drugs and what not." They were right and I think the young woman sensed it. I've never been on the 1L/1M after about 6 p.m. but even during the day, the crew can get a bit rowdy. For a stretch, someone was thrown off the bus nearly every time I rode it. I've seen people cuss the bus driver or fight each other. One man actually threw something at the bus as it pulled away from the curb.

These experiences are less frequent now. With the recent fare increase, the number of homeless men and women on the bus seems substantially fewer than it was and I no longer ride it during peak hours because of my work schedule. But the truth is that I also altered my route as a brazen attempt to avoid homeless people.

Caution is sometimes warranted. Homelessness inherently blurs the line between public and private. A park may be a public space but after dark, you may find yourself wandering through someone's home. Public space becomes private territory. Where there is private territory, there's always the possibility for aggression. The police officer acts in the public interest by enforcing the public nature of city-owned and regulated space. The pushback from the homeless is a defensive action. The homeless have no choice but to appropriate public spaces for themselves as a way of carving out a place in the world. It is literally all they have and the police are a persistent reminder that it isn't really theirs. In a sense, the homeless population of Austin had appropriated the 1L/1M and made it their own. The rest of us were guests. For the most part, we were welcome guests. Disputes between people on the bus were always far less common than disputes between the driver, as the enforcer of public standards of behavior and decency, and some unruly homeless person. It still felt like their space.

But that same sense of ownership was part of Jennifer's demeanor, too. I could sense her feeling of ownership not just of public transportation but of Austin. She wanted the tourists from Salem to feel at home in her city. She appointed herself a one-woman welcome committee. I'm sure there were many reasons but what I sensed was how much she loved Austin and wanted them to have a good experience there. They were painfully out of place. The man wore a polo shirt and a pair of khaki pants and his wife wore carefully pressed capri pants and a floral print blouse. This might not have been out of place in Cedar Park or one of Austin's other suburbs but downtown—and especially on the 1L/1M—they stood out like a sore thumb. Ignoring them because they were different wouldn't have been very Austin and Jennifer Gale was, above all else, real Austin. So she saw to it they had good directions to their destination and a restaurant recommendation. She even provided a little entertainment on the way. These are the actions of a woman at home.

Of course, she got something out of the exchange. With many homeless people, what comes across is a deep sense of loneliness. A few moments of conversation with a stranger is a poor substitute for companionship but it might ease the burden of isolation. In those first days of riding the bus when I was still new to the city and had no friends outside of my immediate family, I looked forward to those brief interludes. I had a bus friend for a little while—a young Vietnamese woman named An who was a student at St. Edward's, where I was teaching. I looked forward to talking with An because she was the only adult conversation I had outside of my household on a regular basis. This is a very human need. I saw the same desire to connect and share in Jennifer and I recognize that I also wanted to connect with her.

What Jennifer offered was more than a few moments of conversation, on the other hand. She established a kind of instant camaraderie with me. Even so, I saw something in her open demeanor and in her conspiratorial air as we interacted with the couple from Salem. She offered a genuine welcome. This true hospitality engendered the friendship we had. In our short time together, I was aware of Jennifer as a living and breathing human person, full of hope and humor, loneliness and pain. This is the reason I felt such a rush of loss when I heard of her death. The affection and humor that pervaded her eulogy was palpable. It set me up for the sting of grief when the story came to its end.

The irony of Jennifer's life is that she was capable of making a random stranger on the bus fall in love with her but she still died alone. She had a tremendous capacity for hospitality and a big, wide-open heart. All that and she died on the steps of a locked church building.

In the midst of life, we are in death. But that day on the bus I saw life, human life shining through the eyes of a lonely woman, and it healed me. In the midst of life death, and in death, new life.

Amma, at the resurrection how shall we rise?

Amma Theodora replied, "As pledge, example, and as prototype we have him who died for us and is risen, Christ our God!"[9]

9. *Sayings*, 84.

chapter nine
Hope

Abba, give me a word.

Abba Pambo said, "If you have a heart, you can be saved."[1]

GOD'S WORK IN THE world is the restoration of humanity. We aren't meant to be anything more or less than human. Our mistake is thinking that being human means making a mess. This may be our common experience but it isn't meant to be the whole truth about who we are. The truth is something bigger and more beautiful.

The converse is that sin is something more profound than our mistakes. In *On the Incarnation,* Athanasius describes sin not as moral failing but as a condition of corruption and death. It is radical in that it reaches the very root of human experience and universal in that it affects every human being. Sin is not breaking the rules. It is futility and corruption. Sin is not human. Sin is death. To paraphrase Paul, the wages of sin is death but the sting of death is sin. Sin arises from our mortality, the futile end to which every life must come. This is not the truth. The truth is that humanity, fully restored, is immortal and incorruptible. Salvation from sin is restoration, healing, a revisioning of the image of God in each human person toward life, health, and peace.

Athanasius uses the evocative image of a painting destroyed by years of neglect and decay. It cannot simply be repaired. It must be repainted. And in order for it to be repainted, a new model needs to sit for the portrait. Where Adam was the original model—created in the image of God and the head of the whole human race—Jesus is the new model. Jesus is a new model, a perfect presentation of the image of God and therefore a perfect image of what is possible for a human being, fully alive and fully restored. Elsewhere, Athanasius implicitly connects this restoration of humanity with the achievement of *apatheia.* The human being, fully

1. *Sayings,* 197.

restored, exists in a state of perfect harmony, where passions are regulated by the will and love is chosen freely and expressed without obstruction.

Athanasius undercuts our comfortable identification between sinful activity and humanity. As I mentioned in an earlier chapter, when we use the phrase, "only human," we're telling ourselves a story about what it means to be a human being. Most of the time, only human covers our sins. Sinning is only human because it's only human to do the wrong thing. We aren't perfect, we tell ourselves. We can't be. It's only human. When we do wrong, we cover it with our humanity as if doing wrong and being a human being went hand in hand. There is a genuine insight in this. Failure is common to human beings. Every single person fails. Anecdotal evidence bears this out. Paul makes it explicit in his letter to the Romans: All have sinned. The experience of meaning well and trying to do right only to fail is one that every person can recognize.

It is not human to sin because it is more human to be divine. This is true at least in a limited sense if we take seriously the Christian insistence that we are created uniquely in the image of God. For Athanasius, reason is the ultimate sign of the image of God in the human person. The passions interfere with the clear exercise of our reason, which is why they have to be regulated. This is a particular and technical way of imagining the relationship between reason and passion—as in the above discussion, it relies on a particular understanding of what a passion is—but the more basic insight is that God's restoration of humanity in the incarnation is not about destroying what is human in order to replace it with something else. It is about restoring humanity to its former glory—a glory fully reflecting the image of God planted in each human person.

Athanasius uses the idea of a marred portrait to illustrate. Christ came as the perfect image of God because the image of God in human beings was being undone. If humanity is a portrait stained beyond recognition, Christ is a new portrait—a true icon—repainted in the same material. Christ is the unity of human and divine natures who is the perfect image of what human beings are meant to be as reflections of the image of God.

This is a both an affirmation of humanity and a challenge. It affirms first the goodness of humanity. Human beings were created good and retain something of that original blessing. We cannot abandon the idea of original sin at this point without creating another conundrum: what about grace? Theological positions that idealize humanity often downplay grace. If we are not fallen, where is the need for grace? If we were born perfect and yet we still sin, we are fully responsible for that sin, just as we are responsible to resist sin of our own efforts. Far from denigrating humanity, the doctrine of original sin acts as a release valve for the pressure of our own expectations for ourselves. Our own efforts to resist sin will always fail. This would be a cause for despair if not for the possibility of grace.

Athanasius's view lends itself to an understanding of grace as a healing agent. The goal of the incarnation is the restoration of humanity—a restoration that begins here and now. This is not the fruit of human effort but rather the fruit of cooperation with the Holy Spirit. It is possible to begin the process of healing our broken humanity. And the more whole, the more human we are. And the more human, the more real.

The stories in this book are about this healing. They are stories about me and a rotating cast of homeless men and women who have moved in and out of my life, on and off the bus. But this is really a story about me and God and the way of meeting God on the bus downtown. It isn't that I see Jesus in the homeless people I encounter. It isn't that pious rush from helping them, as if I were playing Jesus. It's that I meet God in the holy encounter between two human beings. When we meet as equals, eye to eye, and we recognize one another as suffering beings created for love and beauty, God is there.

The moments where I attain that are less common in my life than I would like. There have been far too many times when I have looked at the homeless and failed to see a human being. I consider this a profound failure of my own humanity and a very grave sin. So this book has been a confession of sins, in a way. There are sins I have committed in thought and deed and sins I have committed by failing to act or speak as I should. I confess my sins to God but I do it here so that others can see a vivid picture of what sin is and what it isn't. Sin isn't a spectacular display most of the time. Mostly it's a mundane thing. It's about small things, the kind of things we easily brush aside as meaning nothing. We excuse ourselves and forgive ourselves and reclassify what we do as acceptable. We do this in the name of health but really we're feeding the disease. Sin is hundreds of tiny decisions that add up to a life that is less full and whole than it should be. The desert fathers and mothers have taught me that if you're daunted by the depth of your own sin, you've made a beginning.

I am nothing less than daunted by the deep roots of my own sinfulness. I can account for some of my less admirable tendencies by looking to my personal history with Johnny. At a formative moment in my life,

I internalized certain habits as a way of coping with a brother who was safe but didn't quite seem safe. He was there without fully being there. He was strange without always being that strange. And because of him, I learned a way of being there without being there and of being engaged without really engaging. I learned to keep a mental distance by joking and assigning nicknames. I learned to keep physical distance by habits of avoidance. I learned to come near without ever lowering my guard. I adopted a stance that was fundamentally ambivalent. This does not imply ambiguity. It doesn't mean being unsure of what I feel. It means I am wrenched, habitually, in opposing directions. I am torn between care and a careful disinterest, between identification with the poor and thanking God I'm well and whole.

I come by this particular failing honestly but I still call it a sin. Even if I've done nothing wrong, strictly speaking, I still call this sin. Sin is not only or perhaps even primarily about my own moral failings. I certainly have them but sin is so much bigger than that. It is the insidious, creeping decay that characterizes everything around me. It is a wasting disease that racks my mind and body, my spirit and soul. Sin is not just something I do. It's something I have. Or, rather, it is something that has me. All the brokenness of Johnny's story, all of his pain, and everything ugly that his illness produced in me is part of the disease we all share. It is all sin.

Even if I'm impressed by the weight of this burden, I don't feel guilty. Guilt shouldn't enter the picture at all, in fact, because guilt is not productive. Guilt arises when I ask myself how I, of all people, could do these things that make me experience guilt. The guilt arises from the suggestion that I, of all people, should know better. And if I know better I should do better. This is where the conscience begins to devour me, asking me again and again how this is possible. The truth is, it's perfectly possible. It's not just possible, it's probable. The most likely scenario is that I fall into sin. This is not a scandal. It's not a cataclysmic failure. It's the truth. Guilt becomes a burden when it interferes with my cherished view that I am a spiritual success. The answer is not to minimize the offense or forgive myself for it. The answer is to name it honestly as the truth about me. I screw it up. I screwed it up again because that is what I do.

Telling the truth about who I am puts an end to guilt. The truth starts with the reality that I am in thrall to sin. But although sinning is what I do, it is not who I am. Guilt sinks its teeth in when I construct an image of myself as somehow beyond sin. I have to take that image down and replace it with something honest. But when I acknowledge the truth about my sin, guilt has no more power over me. Incidentally, neither does sin. When I recognize that the way I act is not who I am, I am free to act in some other way.

This would be works righteousness if I thought I could accomplish any of this on my own. Knowing that my actions should be avoided is not enough. I can't do it. I am too caught. The insight that when I fail, my humanity is diminished, is not enough, either. For transformation, two things are necessary: Grace and practice. Grace comes from God but knowledge precedes practice. If sin diminishes my humanity—and I firmly believe that it does—then I am not stuck with it. Once I know that, I can begin again, empowered by the Holy Spirit. This is all very good news. I am not stuck with sin because I am a human being, created in the image of God. When I know that, I can begin again and live like someone who was created for something better than a life of sin.

I am meant for something better than crossing the street to avoid a homeless man. I am meant to do better than leaping off the bus at the first hint of discomfort. I am meant to face people as they are and look past whatever offends me to the truth. And the truth is, the homeless are human beings like me.

Fear and revulsion stand in the way of this better life. I used the term *passion* to describe them here. They are movements of the soul that prompt sinful actions. They are part of my experience of sin. They move me and I act, bypassing whatever love I have rattling around in my brain. Until I learn to recognize them and overcome them, I am completely bound by sin. I am caught in its way of death.

By the power of the Holy Spirit, I am not dead yet. There are signs of life in me and around me. I felt it the day I met Tyrone, called Yaseen. I felt the familiar revulsion but I didn't let it overcome me. I experienced the discomfort but I sat with him anyway and listened to his story. I looked right into his watery yellow eyes and I saw his life. I saw his love for God. I saw pain and loneliness, the emptiness left by the death of his wife. I sat with him and I saw the truth that he was a broken human being. Like me. And I learned his name.

I felt it even stronger the day I met Jennifer Gale—a divine appointment if I've ever experienced one. I felt her energy and her spirit. I saw the way she put the people around her at ease. She concerned herself with their comfort and ignored their reactions to her. She won them over, the way God comes to humanity to win us with the persuasive power of love. I saw her brokenness, too. Her fatigue, her confusion, and her pain were evident. She was a weary person and a dying woman, although neither of us knew it then. Her story burns with the truth that even in the midst of life we are in death. And yet from death comes new life—this time a spark of love in the heart of a young woman who met Jennifer only once. There is hope for me.

I am not alone in my ambivalence about the homeless. I see signs of the same struggle in the people around me and across my city. Austin's love affair with Leslie Cochran speaks to the same uneasy coexistence of attitudes. We love Leslie and embrace him, but not too closely. We want to help him but we also want to respect his space. We enjoy him but maybe not when our kids are around to ask questions about why he wears a skirt or shows people his thong. We love the idea of Leslie but we may never speak to him. We may give him some money but we don't necessarily want to know too much about where he sleeps at night.

But we love still Leslie as a symbol of our hopes. He represents the best things about Austin. He embodies a spirit of creativity and authenticity. It doesn't matter to Leslie if some people think he should wear pants. Leslie is who he is, no compromises. And he's indelibly local. Leslie is part of what makes Austin different from Dallas or Houston. Leslie is part of the fabric of the real Austin we like to talk about. He's part of an Austin where anybody who wants to can feel at home. It doesn't matter if you're weird or you stink. It doesn't matter what people think of you. You're free to create a life for yourself. This is what makes Austin what it is.

I take our love for Leslie as a sign that there is hope for us. We see the broken and the weird and we love it anyway, just as it is. We make a cathedral out of junk and a hero out of a homeless transvestite. Austin is a world upside down, which means it's a world open to the new. New hopes, new life. Leslie is a sign of life amid the wreckage of our broken human community. He's the sign of a promise. There is hope for us after all, Austin. We have hearts. There is hope for a new beginning, every day a fresh start, every day a new chance to be real. We can be saved.

BIBLIOGRAPHY

Alfeyev, Hilarion. *The Spiritual World of Isaac the Syrian*. Kalamazoo, MI: Cistercian Publications, 2000.

Armstrong, Karen. *The Spiral Staircase: My Climb Out of Darkness*. New York: Anchor, 2005.

Athanasius. *The Life of Anthony and the Letter to Marcellinus*. Translated by Robert C. Gregg. The Classics of Western Spirituality. Mahwah, NJ: Paulist, 1980.

———. *On the Incarnation: The Treatise De Incarnatione Verbi Dei*. Translated and edited by a Religious of C.S.M.V. Crestwood, NY: St. Vladimir's Seminary Press, 1996.

Bondi, Roberta. *To Love as God Loves: Conversations with the Early Church*. Minneapolis: Fortress, 1987.

Brown, Peter. "The Rise and Function of the Holy Man in Late Antiquity, 1971-1997." *Journal of Early Christian Studies* 6 (1998) 353-76.

———. "The Rise and Function of the Holy Man in Late Antiquity." *Journal of Roman Studies* 61 (1971) 80-101.

Burden of Dreams. DVD. Directed by Les Blank. 1982. Irvington, NY: The Criterion Collection. 2005.

Burton-Christie, Douglas. *The Word in the Desert: Scripture and the Quest for Holiness in Early Monasticism*. New York: Oxford University Press, 1993.

Chitty, Derwas. *The Desert a City: An Introduction to the Study of Egyptian and Palestinian Monasticism Under the Christian Empire*. Crestwood, NY: St. Vladimir's Seminary Press, 1977.

Dawes, Elizabeth, and Norman Hepburn Baynes. *Three Byzantine Saints: Contemporary Biographies of St. Daniel the Stylite, St. Theodore of Sykeon, and St. John the Almsgiver*. Crestwood, NY: St. Vladimir's Seminary Press, 1977.

Donizetti, Gaetano. *Lucia di Lammermoor*. Joan Sutherland, Alfredo Kraus, Pablo Elvira, Paul Plishka, Richard Bonynge. DVD. 1983. Metropolitan Opera. Hamburg, Germany: Deutsche Grammophon, 2006.

Donizetti, Gaetano. *Lucia di Lammermoor*. Anna Netrebko, Piotr Beczala, Mariusz Kwiecien, Ildar Abdrazakov. DVD. Metropolitan Opera. Hamburg, Germany: Deutsche Grammophon, 2009.

Donnie Darko. DVD. Directed by Richard Kelly. 2001. Century City, CA.: 20th Century Fox. 2007.

Doran, Robert. *The Lives of Simeon Stylites*. Kalamazoo, MI: Cistercian Publications, 1989.

Elm, Susanna. *Virgins of God: The Making of Asceticism in Late Antiquity*. New York: Oxford University Press, 1996.

Evagrius, Ponticus. *The Praktikos and Chapters on Prayer*. Translated by John Eudes Bamberger OCSO. Kalamazoo, MI: Cistercian Publications, 1981.

Farley, Wendy. *The Wounding and Healing of Desire: Weaving Heaven and Earth*. Louisville: Westminster, 2005.

Mathewes-Green, Frederica. *Facing East: A Pilgrim's Journey into the Mysteries of Orthodoxy*. San Francisco: HarperOne, 2006.

Napoleon Dynamite. Directed by Jared Hess. 2004. Century City, CA.: 20th Century Fox. 2004.

The Sayings of the Desert Fathers: The Alphabetical Collection. Translated by Benedicta Ward SLG. Kalamazoo, MI: Cistercian Publications, 2006.

Schmemann, Alexander. *For the Life of the World: Sacraments and Orthodoxy*. 2nd ed. Crestwood, NY: St. Vladimir's Seminary Press, 1997.

Sider, Ronald J. *Good News and Good Works: A Theology for the Whole Gospel*. Grand Rapids: Baker, 1999.

Steinke, Darcey. *Easter Everywhere: A Memoir*. New York: Bloomsbury, 2008.